NARNIA BECKONS

C. S. LEWIS'S THE LION, THE WITCH AND THE WARDROBE AND BEYOND

NARNIA BECKONS

C. S. LEWIS'S THE LION, THE WITCH AND THE WARDROBE AND BEYOND

TED BAEHR ∞ JAMES BAEHR

with illustrations by Angela West

BROADMAN
& HOLMAN
PUBLISHERS

NASHVILLE, TENNESSEE

NARNIA BECKONS

Copyright © 2005 by Theodore Baehr

All rights reserved.

Published by Broadman & Holman Publishers

Nashville, Tennessee

ISBN 13: 978-0-8054-4042-3

ISBN 10: 0-8054-4042-9

Dewey Decimal Classification: 791.43

Subject Heading: MOTION PICTURES—PRODUCTION AND DIRECTION

LEWIS, C. S. (CLIVE STAPLES). LION, THE WITCH AND THE WARDROBE

Printed in China

1 2 3 4 08 07 06 05

Special thanks to The Kilns and CSL Foundation for allowing the authors to visit their sites. Photographs by: Lili Baehr, The Wade Center, Robert Cording, Evy Baehr.
All illustrations in this book are the property of Broadman & Holman Publishers and may not be reproduced without permission.
Illustration on page 89: Emilie Goddard; page 146: Robert Cording. All other Narnia character illustrations were created by Angela West.
Mrs. West loves to create art in all types of media and can be reached at her email address: mawagd@yahoo.com.

DEDICATION

With love and great thanksgiving:

Ted Baehr dedicates this book:
To our Lord and Savior Jesus Christ,
And, to Lili, Peirce, Jim, Robby, Evy, and all of whom contributed to the book.

James Baehr dedicates this book:
To my family, whose support has enriched my life beyond my ability to repay.
To my friends, who have believed and supported me, despite all evidence to the contrary.
To my God, for whom I strive to live and without whom I see no reason to draw breath.

Also, we want to thank: David Shepherd, Len Goss, Kim Overcash, Diana Lawrence, Chip MacGregor, Tom & Katie Ward,
Peter Cousin, Cindy Heiskell, directors, supporters, friends, and all the wonderful contributors and friends of this project.

To go deeper and for more great articles, insights, information, and reflections by some of the best C. S. Lewis scholars, please go to www.movieguide.org.
With proof of purchase of Narnia Beckons, you will be able to access more great articles and insights into The Lion, the Witch and the Wardrobe.

Please note that the ownership of The Chronicles of Narnia *copyright and trademark belongs to the C. S. Lewis Estate*
and C. S. Lewis's publishers, and the commentaries herein represent a fair use of that material.

CONTENTS

Father in heaven,

Thank you that all creation testifies to you!

Thank you for giving us the good news of new life available
to each of us through your Son, Jesus the Christ.

Thank you for giving us your Holy Spirit, our teacher.

Bless all who read this book—
may they come to know you and make you known.

Grant us, as your people, wisdom, knowledge and understanding.

Help us to reveal your Word to those in need.

Help us to lift up your holy name, Jesus,
through the power of your Holy Spirit.

Amen.

I spoke through the prophets
and granted many visions;
I gave parables through the prophets.

—Hosea 12:10

*T*he creation itself will be liberated from its bondage to decay
and brought into the glorious freedom of the children of God. —ROMANS 8:21 (NIV)

EDMUND, PETER, LUCY, & SUSAN

ONCE UPON A TIME

> FOR NOW WE SEE THROUGH A GLASS, DARKLY; BUT THEN FACE TO FACE: NOW I KNOW IN PART; BUT THEN SHALL I KNOW EVEN AS ALSO I AM KNOWN.
>
> —*1 CORINTHIANS 13:12* (KJV)

Back in 1980, when I was president of the organization that produced The Chronicles of Narnia: *The Lion, the Witch and the Wardrobe* on CBS television, I received a letter from a middle-aged gentleman who said that his wife had been witnessing to him about Jesus and his atonement for years, but he just couldn't understand the concept until he saw the animated *The Lion, the Witch and the Wardrobe* on CBS television. He suddenly understood and accepted Jesus Christ as his Lord and Savior.

This was one of many letters about how the Emmy Award-winning television special impacted the thirty-seven million people who saw it.

Just as *The Lion, the Witch and the Wardrobe* was wrapping production in the late 1970s, the founder of the organization, who struggled for twenty-six years to produce it, was unceremoniously removed from office, and I was hired to finish the marketing of the television program.

Although the animation now is washed out, the TV movie is still powerful. The power of the story derives from the storyteller C. S. Lewis, who not only loved to tell stories but also was an expert in logic. These two gifts combined to make him the most formidable Christian apologist of the twentieth century. He asked the right questions, analyzed the answers, and transformed the answers into stories that still change lives.

JUST FOR YOU

This book will help you gain greater insight into C. S. Lewis's, The Chronicles of Narnia: *The Lion, the Witch and the Wardrobe*, and your own faith and values. In this book many of the leading C. S. Lewis scholars and experts will: (1) give you an overview of who C. S. Lewis was; (2) reflect on the depth of meanings in The Chronicles of Narnia; and (3) examine *The Lion, the Witch and the Wardrobe*, including the TV and movie productions based on this classic story. Also, this book will provide you with an inspirational journey through the book that will help you know the true Lion King so you can grow in faith, knowledge, discernment, and wisdom. As such, *Narnia Beckons* is filled with readable, practical, and illuminating truths, tools, and tips to help you develop a deeper relationship with God and a greater understanding of his grace.

This book presents an introduction. It is full of articles by experts but presents the lay point of view that C. S. Lewis, who liked to be called Jack, loved so much.

In the PBS television documentary, *The Magic Never Ends*, C. S. Lewis expert Walter Hooper makes the brilliant observation that Lewis "provided not just a glimpse of truth, he really gave readers the big picture. While in other writers you get a corner of the curtain . . . raised, you get a little bit of the truth, with Lewis the big curtains just open up wide, and they extend all the way to the side of the theater and you see everything that is in front of you."[1]

C. S. Lewis was born and reared in Ireland, which has produced many great writers, and spent hours in imaginative play with his brother. He studied at one of the finest universities in England, Oxford, and became a great scholar. Several of his books on literature are still the best that have ever been written. Because his mother died when he was young and he suffered the loss of his best friend on the battlefield in World War I, he rejected God. Only after hours of discussion with J. R. R. Tolkien, Hugo Dyson, and other Oxford friends did he come to realize the truth of the gospel.

This arduous, intellectual conversion made him a formidable apologist to the unconverted at a time when England had become a post-Christian culture. With uncanny insight he made the case for the gospel in terms that won millions of believers.

BELOVED STORIES

His Chronicles of Narnia books sell more copies now than they did when first published. Sixty million readers have discovered the wonderful world of Narnia since C. S. Lewis created *The Lion, the Witch and the Wardrobe* over fifty years ago. It is one of the most popular books ever written and has been produced as a television special and a major motion picture.

These books have helped millions of people to know Jesus Christ even though Lewis did not intend them as allegories in the strict sense of the term. Instead, he argued that they were "supposals" and that he was merely supposing what would happen if God came to another world.

The Lion, the Witch and the Wardrobe remains popular because it resonates with every one of us who seeks forgiveness for our mistakes and a new life. Out of his love for myth and his faith, C. S. Lewis crafted a superb story that has become a classic children's tale.

DEEPER MAGIC

Some Christians are disturbed by C. S. Lewis's use of the word *magic* in The Chronicles of Narnia. Magic is forbidden in the Bible. Revelation 21:8 makes clear that "those who practice magic arts, the idolaters and all liars—their place will be in the fiery lake of burning sulfur" (NIV).

As one of the articles in this book explains, C. S. Lewis made clear in his novels that it is wrong to use magic, especially for personal gain, but even when people do such an evil thing, there is a deeper magic

The Bible teaches that "all of the creation itself will be liberated from its bondage to decay and brought into the glorious freedom of the children of God."

—ROMANS 8:21
(NIV)

THE WHITE WITCH

(or law) written into the creation by the Creator to right the wrongs.

The Bible teaches that all of "the creation itself will be liberated from its bondage to decay and brought into the glorious freedom of the *children of God*" (Rom. 8:21 NIV, author emphasis). Throughout the centuries, with this principle in mind, the church has redeemed and reinvested ancient ceremonies, holidays, and devices with Christian meaning and content.

Thus, both C. S. Lewis and Tolkien reinvested the word *magic* with redemptive meaning. In The Chronicles of Narnia, Lewis uses *magic* as a synonym for laws that God has written into the universe. Although the stories by Lewis are fantasy, they should not be confused with the world of the occult. The worlds Lewis and Tolkien created are real worlds with real consequences and real hope.

One of the essential building blocks of any theology or philosophy is ontology, which simply means the nature of the ground of being or the essence of the world in which we live. For a Hindu and most occultists, people live in an imaginary world, a great thought, an illusion. Christians and Jews, however, live in a real world with real pain and real suffering, a world that needs a real God and real salvation.

For a Christian, therefore, things are real, and, as shown in *The Lion, the Witch and the Wardrobe*, actions have consequences. When Edmund succumbs to the temptations of the white witch, he has to pay the consequences, or someone has to pay in his stead.

In contrast, with their occult, nomenalistic ontology, the *Harry Potter* books propose that the world can be manipulated through magic. Things change shape; nothing is really real. Therefore, there is no need for a savior; one has merely to have the right incantations or think the right thoughts to be saved. Thus, the individual shapes the world and is in that sense a god.

WHAT DIFFERENCE DOES ONTOLOGY MAKE?

The nature of reality makes a world of difference. Mother Teresa saw the poor and dying on the streets of Calcutta as real people and started rescuing the sick and taking care of them. The Hindus saw them as just Maya, or the World of Illusion, and were confused and offended when she took care of the sick and dying.

The good news is that the Creator, who created reality, is ready to rescue us from our fallen world. In his world, life has meaning. Rescued by God through Jesus Christ's sacrificial death, we are safe to build a civilization.

NOTHING WILL BE ABLE TO SEPARATE US FROM THE LOVE OF GOD THAT IS IN CHRIST JESUS OUR LORD.

—ROMANS 8:39 (NIV)

Theology means simply the study of or knowledge of God, and he calls all of us to know him and make him known.

One of the reasons these arguments are raging is that the church has drifted away from a solid understanding of trinitarian theology toward an eclectic theology that has adopted all sorts of unbiblical doctrines and has become lukewarm about biblical truth. That's why the Battle for People's Souls, and the Battle Between Good and Evil, is really just a Battle for Biblical Truth.

Everyone has a theology concerning the Bible. Even those who deny that the Bible is God's inerrant Word, or who proclaim that the Bible isn't true, are proclaiming a particular worldview and theology about the Bible, its truth, and its applicability to the affairs of man.

Ultimately, as C. S. Lewis stated, there is no neutrality concerning God, the Bible, truth, Jesus Christ, the nature of being (or ontology), and good and evil. We are all responsible for our theology. We are faced with three questions: How should we decide what to believe? By what authority? By what standard?

As Paul states in 2 Timothy 3:10–17, the Bible is a wonderful authority, a great standard that, when read and studied, can point us toward right thinking and thoroughly equip us "for every good work." The Bible convinces us and convicts us. As such, it shows us, beyond a shadow of a doubt, that it is far better to be like Mother Teresa or C. S. Lewis rather than those who ignore the spiritually and materially poor because they place no trust in God.

And, though we may be persecuted by "evil men and imposters" who "go from bad to worse, deceiving and being deceived" (2 Tim. 3:13 NIV), we can know with certainty that nothing "will be able to separate us from the love of God that is in Christ Jesus our Lord" (Rom. 8:39 NIV). That is the ground of difference between the Christian and the non-Christian.

THE REST OF THE STORY

Although Lewis did not intend to give a one-to-one correlation to the gospel of Jesus Christ, *The Lion, the Witch and the Wardrobe* is a compelling allegory that leads the reader to a deeper understanding of the good news. Through it Lewis brings to life the critical verse in Scripture: "God so loved the world that He gave His only begotten Son, that whoever believes in Him should not perish but have everlasting life" (John 3:16 NKJV).

In the book the lion Aslan, son of the emperor-beyond-the-sea, gives his life to pay the death penalty for a human boy, Edmund, who became a traitor to his family and to all that was good in Narnia. Edmund is to be put to death for betraying his family by joining the company of the evil white witch in order to gorge himself on Turkish delight.

Aslan rescues Edmund by dying in Edmund's place. Edmund is set free, and Aslan is resurrected! Transformed by the love that Aslan showed him, Edmund joins the company of Aslan for the good of Narnia.

INSPIRATION

C. S. Lewis's book is inspired by a true story. Two thousand years ago Jesus sacrificed his life to pay the penalty of humanity's betrayal of God. He is the son of the true God. We all, like Edmund, have betrayed God by rebelling against him. We all, like Edmund, deserve a death penalty for our betrayal. But Jesus, through his sacrifice, rescued us by dying in our place. If we trust in him, we are set free, transformed by his love to join God's company for the good of our world.

"The Scripture declares that the whole world is a prisoner of sin" (Gal. 3:22 NIV). Sin is the condition of man and sets man's will above God's. A listen to the morning news shows demonstrates with clarity just how destructive sin is. Daily people add to the brokenness in our world by choosing,

Aslan

God so loved the world
that He gave His only begotten Son,
that whoever believes Him
should not perish but have
everlasting life.

—JOHN 3:16

EDMUND

ALL HAVE SINNED AND FALL SHORT OF THE GLORY OF GOD.
—ROMANS 3:23

like Edmund, to do what feels right to them. But sin isn't only a problem for characters in novels and people in the newspapers, it is a problem for all of us, you included. "All have sinned and fall short of the glory of God" (Rom. 3:23). Stop and think over your day: whose desires were the most important in the decisions you made? If the answer is not God, you have a problem with sin. The good news, however, is that God has made a way for you to be set free from bondage to sin and death.

In *The Lion, the Witch and the Wardrobe,* C. S. Lewis dramatizes the war between good and evil. Aslan won his battle through the sacrifice of his own life, and by doing so he was resurrected. Just so, Jesus Christ won the battle when he gave his life to save us and was resurrected. The real battle rages inside each of us, and we are victorious only when we accept the sacrifice Jesus paid to redeem us. Once we are saved we become like Edmund, transformed by God's love and ready to join his family for the good of our world.

The Bible speaks of how much God loves us and wants us to be transformed: "God showed his great love for us by sending Christ to die for us while we were still sinners" (Rom. 5:8 NLT). He loves each of us in spite of our betrayal of him as sinners. In fact, God's love is powerful enough to redeem us from our death penalty.

Narnia Beckons

Here is a simple prayer you may pray to respond to God's love for you:

Lord Jesus,

thank you for dying on earth to save me

and for being resurrected to give me new life.

I believe you died for me and all the wrongs I have

committed. I believe that you were buried, rose again,

and ascended into heaven, and I accept your free gift

of salvation and new life in your company.

Amen.

More Great Articles & Insights

To go deeper and for more great articles, insights, information, and reflections by some of the best C. S. Lewis scholars, go to www.movieguide.org. With proof of purchase of *Narnia Beckons*, you will be able to access more great insights into *The Lion, the Witch and the Wardrobe*. Some of the outstanding articles on the private, members-only section of www.movieguide.org Web site are:

"Imagine That! Narnia, Middle-Earth, and the Faith Formation of Today's Teenagers" by Sarah Arthur, best-selling author of *Walking with Frodo* (Thirsty Books) and *Walking with Bilbo* (Tyndale).

"Wardrobes in Worlds: The Divergent Visions of C. S. Lewis and Philip Pullman" by James S. C. Baehr.

"Nurturing Glory and Wonder: Teaching the Chronicles of Narnia in the Church" by Perry C. Bramlett, author of *C. S. Lewis: Life at the Center* (Peake Road), *Touring C. S. Lewis' Ireland and England* (Smyth & Helwys), and coauthor of *A C. S. Lewis Spiritual Reader* (forthcoming).

"Journey: One Man's Faith Brings Lewis' World to Life" by Robert Cording, president of Questar Pictures, Inc.

"The Childhood Shows the Man . . ." by Ruth James Cording, author of *C. S. Lewis—a Celebration of His Early Life* (Broadman & Holman).

"The True Myth" by Chip Duncan, Emmy Award-winning documentary film-maker and author of *The Magic Never Ends—The Life and Work of C. S. Lewis* (W Publishing Group).

"Beyond the Wardrobe: Where Big Gifts Come in Small Packages" by Karen Erkel and Debby Edwards.

"Teacher Historian Critic Apologist" by Dabney Hart, professor at Georgia State University.

"C. S. Lewis on Stage" by Tom Key, executive artistic director of Atlanta's acclaimed Theatrical Outfit.

"Into the Land of the Imagination" by Clyde Kilby, author of *Images of Salvation in the Fiction of C. S. Lewis* (Harold Shaw Publishers) and *The Christian World of C. S. Lewis* (Eerdmans).

"Western Civilization at the Crossroads" by Peter Kreeft, professor at Boston College and the author of *C. S. Lewis, Heaven, the Heart's Deepest Longing; Between Heaven and Hell* (InterVarsity Press); and *Yes or No* (Ignatius).

"Embalmed Images: C. S. Lewis and the Art of Film" by Terry Lindvall, professor at Regent University and author of *The Surprise of Laughter: C. S. Lewis and the Comic Spirit* (Nelson).

"The Good Guys and the Bad Guys: Teachable Moments in The Chronicles of Narnia" by Louis Markos, professor at Houston Baptist University and author of *Lewis Agonistes: How C. S. Lewis Can Train Us to Wrestle with the Modern and Postmodern World* (Broadman & Holman).

"The Assumptions of Narnia" by Paul McCusker, author of the recently released *The Mill House* (Zondervan) and the dramatist of all seven Chronicles of Narnia for *Focus on the Family Radio Theatre*.

"The Healing of Harms: C. S. Lewis' Philosophy of Healing" by The Rev. Canon Mark Pearson, a priest and author of the widely acclaimed book *Christian Healing: A Practical and Comprehensive Guide* (Charisma).

"Into the Light" by G. P. Taylor, an English clergyman and international best-selling author of *Shadowmancer* (Putnam), *Wormwood* (Putnam), and *Tersias*.

"Further Up and Further In" by Will Vaus, author of *Mere Theology: A Guide to the Thought of C. S. Lewis* (InterVarsity Press).

Endnote:

1. John Ryan Duncan, *The Magic Never Ends: The Life and Work of C. S. Lewis* (Nashville: W Publishing Group, 2001), 181.

PART I

IN THE BEGINNING—
C. S. LEWIS

y debt to him is very great, my reverence to him undiminished.

—C. S. Lewis, writing in *Surprised by Joy* about his tutor, W. T. Kirkpatrick

Professor Kirk

C. S. Lewis: A Profile of His Life

Lyle Dorsett

Lyle W. Dorsett was curator of the Marion E. Wade Collection, which houses C. S. Lewis's original manuscripts, letters, and papers at Wheaton College, Wheaton, Illinois. He is the author of *Seeking the Secret Place: The Spiritual Formation of C. S. Lewis, And God Came In: The Extraordinary Story of Joy Davidman, Her Life and Marriage to C. S. Lewis,* and many other books, and coeditor of *C. S. Lewis, Letters to Children.* This article first appeared in issue 7 of *Christian History* magazine, and is used by permission.

"I'm tall, fat, rather bald, red-faced, double-chinned, black-haired, have a deep voice, and wear glasses for reading," C. S. Lewis wrote to a young admirer in 1954. If the famous author had been prone to notice clothing, he might have added that his trousers were usually in dire need of pressing, his jackets threadbare and blemished by snags and food spots, and his shoes scuffed and worn at the heels.

> There were books in the study, books in the dining room, books in the cloakroom, books (two deep) in the great bookcase on the landing, books in a bedroom, books piled as high as my shoulder in the cistern attic, books of all kinds.
>
> —C. S. Lewis, in *Surprised by Joy*

But, Jack, as C. S. Lewis's friends knew him, was not bothered by fashion. It is known that he was slovenly. On the contrary, he was meticulous about the precise use of words, the quality of evidence presented in arguments, and the meter in verse. Nevertheless, the style and condition of personal attire was near the bottom of his list of concerns, whereas books and ideas were among his top priorities.

Early Influences

Lewis was born into a bookish family of Protestants in Belfast, Ireland, on November 29, 1898. His father, Albert, and his mother, Florence Augusta Hamilton, possessed first-rate minds, and they were members of the Church of Ireland. Eclectic in their reading tastes, they purchased and read many books, and their love for the printed word was passed on to their children. Jack and Warren (his only sibling, three years his senior) were he remembered, and none were off-limits to him. On rainy days—and there were many in northern Ireland—he pulled volumes off the shelves and entered into worlds created by authors such as Conan Doyle, E. Nesbit, Mark Twain, and Henry Wadsworth Longfellow.

After brother Warnie was sent off to boarding school in England, Jack became somewhat reclusive. He spent more time in books and an imaginary world of "dressed animals" and "knights in armor." But he did more than read books; he wrote and illustrated his own stories as well.

C. S. "Jack" Lewis and his brother Warren as boys.

not only read to aloud and taught to read; they were encouraged to use the large family library.

In his autobiography, *Surprised by Joy,* C. S. Lewis recalled early memories of "endless books." "There were books in the study, books in the dining room, books in the cloakroom, books (two deep) in the great bookcase on the landing, books in a bedroom, books piled as high as my shoulder in the cistern attic, books of all kinds,"

One of Jack's childhood drawings.

If Warren Lewis's exile across the Irish Sea to school in 1905 drove Jack further into himself and books, his mother's death from cancer in 1908 made him even more withdrawn. Mrs. Lewis's death came just three months prior to Jack's tenth birthday, and the young man was hurt deeply by her passing. Not only did he lose a mother; his father never fully recovered from her death. For many years thereafter, both boys felt estranged from their father, and home life was never warm and satisfying again.

The death of Mrs. Lewis convinced young Jack that the God he encountered in church and in the Bible his mother gave him was, if not cruel, at least a vague abstraction. Four or five years later, by 1911 or 1912, and with the additional influence of a spiritually unorthodox boarding school matron, Lewis forsook Christianity and became an avowed atheist.

By autumn 1914, C. S. Lewis was somewhat adrift. He had lost his faith and his mother, and he felt alienated from his father. He was extremely close to his brother, but they saw each other only on holidays. A new

University College at Oxford, where Lewis studied as a young man.

friendship was beginning with a fellow student, Arthur Greeves, but it was interrupted in September when C. S. Lewis was sent to Great Bookham, Surrey, to be privately tutored by W. T. Kirkpatrick, a brilliant teacher and friend of Lewis's father.

"The Great Knock," as the Lewis family dubbed Mr. Kirkpatrick, had a profound effect upon the youth. He introduced him to the classics in Greek, Latin, and Italian literature and helped him make a beginning in German. Kirkpatrick not only led Lewis to great books; he pushed him to understand them in the original languages.

A most demanding tutor, Kirkpatrick helped Jack learn how to criticize and analyze; and he taught him how to think, speak, and write logically. Consequently, after nearly three years with Kirkpatrick, C. S. Lewis was tough-minded and widely read. Many years later, Lewis wrote in *Surprised by Joy* that "my debt to him is very great, my reverence to this day undiminished."

The debt was large indeed. Kirkpatrick helped the young man prepare for scholarship examinations at Oxford, and the demanding mentor played no small role in Lewis's outstanding performance at University College, where he took highest honors in Honour Moderations, Greats, and English in 1920, 1922, and 1923 respectively.

If Kirkpatrick taught Lewis to think critically—to demand evidence for even the most casual assertions—Oxford introduced him to a wide horizon of ideas. Whereas Lewis's hard-pressing mentor had helped reinforce his atheism, a few associates at Oxford forced him to reexamine his belief in a universe without God.

The famous Bodleian Library, Oxford.

❧ OXFORD YEARS

Lewis entered the world of Oxford in 1917 as a student, and he never really left. Despite an interruption to fight in World War I and his professorship at Cambridge beginning in 1955, he always maintained his home and friends in Oxford. He loved the bookshops, the pubs, and the Bodleian Library, and he reveled in the company of local men who loved to read, write, and discuss books. His attachment to Oxford was so strong that when he taught at Cambridge from 1955 to 1963 he commuted back to Oxford on weekends so that he could be close to familiar places and beloved friends.

It was in Oxford that Lewis pursued things of the mind with fervor. Ideas, books, and debates were ordinary fare in this heady environment. With no particular purpose in life beyond stimulating his imagination, feeding his intellectual curiosity, and writing for publication and posterity, he thoroughly enjoyed academic life. In 1919 he published his first book, a cycle of lyrics entitled *Spirits in Bondage*, which he wrote under the pseudonym Clive Hamilton. In 1924 he became a philosophy tutor at University College. Then in 1925 he was elected a Fellow of Magdalen College, where he tutored in English language and literature. The next year his second volume of poetry, *Dymer*, was published under the name Clive Hamilton.

Above: The Sheldonian Theatre, next to the Bodleian Library.
Below: Bridge of Sighs, Oxford.

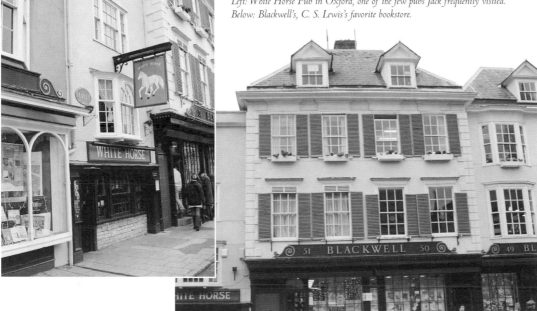

Left: White Horse Pub in Oxford, one of the few pubs Jack frequently visited.
Below: Blackwell's, C. S. Lewis's favorite bookstore.

Alongside the generally self-centered life Lewis was leading, he demonstrated a loyal and generous nature. When his college roommate, Paddy Moore, was killed in World War I, Jack befriended Paddy's mother, Mrs. Janie King Moore, and her adolescent daughter Maureen. Then in 1920, after completing his first degree, Lewis decided to share lodgings with them so that he could more carefully look out for their needs.

Above: The streets of Oxford, where Lewis walked daily.

Left: C. S. Lewis's first boarding house in Oxford.

Spiritual Awakening

This gesture of kindness did more than help Mrs. Moore and Maureen; it got C. S. Lewis outside of himself and taught him patience. The association with the Moores also introduced him to Mrs. Moore's brother, a combat veteran who suffered from a severe war-inflicted nervous disorder. This personal encounter apparently shook Lewis's confidence in materialism, because a letter he wrote in 1923 to his friend Arthur Greeves suggests a slight spiritual awakening. It seems that "Doc," as the Moores and Lewis referred to him, came to stay with the trio for three weeks. During the visit Doc underwent an ordeal of extreme mental torture. After the attack, when the poor wretch was hospitalized, Lewis wrote to his friend that Doc had believed he was in hell. He wore out his body in the "awful mental tortures" and then died from heart failure—"unconscious at the end thank God." Lewis concluded his observation by suggesting it is "a damned world—and we once thought we could be happy with books and music!"

The spiritual awakening continued, enhanced by reading books by George MacDonald and G. K. Chesterton. One MacDonald volume called *Phantastes* had a powerful impact on his thinking. "What it actually did to me," wrote Lewis, "was

to convert, even to baptize . . . my imagination." At Oxford Lewis continued to read MacDonald, and he imbibed G. K. Chesterton as well. The latter author's books, especially *The Everlasting Man*, raised serious questions about the young intellectual's materialism.

While MacDonald and Chesterton were stirring Lewis's thoughts, a close friend, Owen Barfield, with whom he spent much time during and after their student years, pounced on the logic of Jack Lewis's atheism. Barfield became a theist and then a Christian, and he frequently badgered Lewis about his materialism. So did Nevill Coghill, a fellow student and lifelong friend who was brilliant yet was, to Lewis's amazement, "a Christian and a thorough-going supernaturalist."

Soon after joining the English faculty at Magdalen College, Lewis met two more Christians, Hugo Dyson and J. R. R. Tolkien. These men soon became close friends of Lewis.

He admired their brilliance and their logic. Soon Lewis recognized that most of his friends, like his favorite authors—MacDonald, Chesterton, Johnson, Spenser, and Milton—held to this Christian angle of vision that threatened his whole worldview.

Gradually during the 1920s, two paths were converging in Lewis's mind: one was reason, the other intuition. In 1929 these roads met, and C. S. Lewis surrendered and admitted that "God was God, and knelt and prayed." Within two years the reluctant convert admitted that Jesus Christ is the Son of God—God incarnate. With this revelation the Oxford don became a communicant in the Church of England.

Magdalen College, Oxford: Jack's faculty room was in the middle section of the second floor where he often looked out at the deer park.

Courtyard view at Magdalen College, Oxford.

A New Life

Christian history shows that when men and women meet Jesus, recognize his nature, and then decide to trust and follow him, they become strikingly different people. Those who convert—who turn around and obey Christ's command to "follow me"— are clearly people with changed lives.

If evidence of conversion is a new life, C. S. Lewis was obviously a believer after 1931. Many changes were apparent. His life now had a purpose—to know and obey God.

This came to fruition most demonstrably in his writing. Earlier efforts to become a poet were laid to rest. The new Christian devoted his talent and energy to writing prose that reflected his recently found faith. Within two years of his conversion, Lewis published *The Pilgrim's Regress: An Allegorical Apology for Christianity, Reason and Romanticism.* This little volume opened a thirty-year stream of books on Christian apologetics and discipleship that became a lifelong avocation. Between 1933 and his death in 1963, C. S. Lewis wrote books including the seven-volume Chronicles of Narnia, *The Screwtape Letters, The Great Divorce,* and *Mere Christianity,* that nudged atheists and agnostics toward the faith, and encouraged and nurtured believers.

As a good steward and responsible professional, Lewis did not ignore his academic discipline. He wrote literary history and criticism such as *The Allegory of Love: A Study in Medieval Tradition, Rehabilitations and Other Essays,* and *English Literature in the Sixteenth Century, Excluding Drama.* These books are still widely read and highly regarded.

Despite the large quantity and high quality of his academic publications, Lewis became known as a literary evangelist. The tone and impact of his theological and apologetical books help account for this reputation, as does his own assertion in a rejoinder to his critic, Dr. W. N. Pittenger, published in *The Christian Century* November 26, 1958, where Lewis admitted that most of what he wrote "is evangelistic."

A Growing Reputation

If Christianity altered Lewis's writing habits, the publication of those books had a palpable effect on his personal life. First of all, the change was manifested in the mail. Once Lewis's books became popular, which they did by the 1940s, he was inundated by letters. Because the famous author believed it was God's will for him to answer most of this mail himself, and because he was convinced, as he said in "The Weight of Glory," that there are "no ordinary people," he took time to write with care to each correspondent regardless of age, education, or place in society. This enterprise consumed many hours each week.

It is common knowledge that Lewis's "Christian" books caused so much disapproval that he was more than once passed over for a professorship at Oxford, with the honors going to men of lesser reputation. It was Magdalene College at Cambridge University that finally honored Lewis with a chair in 1955 and thereby recognized his original and important contributions to English literary history and criticism.

Along with Lewis's international reputation, ever-growing royalties, and thousands of fans throughout the English-speaking world, came increasing alienation. Did Lewis take comfort in his Lord's warning in the Sermon on the Mount that his disciples would indeed be insulted and persecuted? We do not know.

Lewis died at The Kilns on November 22, 1963. He is buried beside his brother, who lived ten more years, in the cemetery of Holy Trinity Church, Headington Quarry, Oxford. His letters and books, and the lives these writings touch, are his legacy.

The cemetery of the Holy Trinity Church, where C. S. Lewis is buried.

C. S. Lewis Chronology

1898   November 29, born in Belfast, Ireland.

1905   Moves to "Little Lea."

1913   Enters Malvern College, England.

1917   April: Begins studies at University College, Oxford.

        September: Commissioned as second lieutenant in Somerset Light Infantry.

        November: Leaves for front lines.

1918   Wounded in action. Returns to hospital in England.

1919   Returns to University College. Publishes first book, *Spirits in Bondage*, a small volume of lyric poems,
        under the name Clive Hamilton.

1925   Elected to a fellowship in English language and literature at Magdalen College, Oxford.

1929   Confesses that "God is God."

1930   Purchases and moves into The Kilns.

1931   Comes to faith in Christ.

1939   Publishes *Out of the Silent Planet*, first book of the Space Trilogy.

1940   First weekly meeting of the Inklings. Publishes *The Problem of Pain*.

1941   Begins a series of radio talks over the BBC.

1942   Publishes *The Screwtape Letters*.

1945   Publishes *The Great Divorce*.

1950   Receives first letter from Joy Davidman Gresham. Publishes *The Lion, the Witch and the Wardrobe*, the first of the Narnian stories.

1952   Meets Joy Davidman Gresham. Publishes *Mere Christianity*.

1955   Leaves Oxford for professorship of Medieval and Renaissance Literature at Magdalen College, Cambridge.

1956   Publishes *Till We Have Faces*, the book Lewis considers his best fictional work. Publishes *The Last Battle*, last of the Narnian series.

        April: Marries Joy Davidman Gresham in a legal ceremony.

        November: Marries Joy in ecclesiastical ceremony at her bedside.

1960   Joy Lewis dies, July 13.

1963   November 22, C. S. Lewis dies (the same day President John F. Kennedy is assassinated).

Source: This article first appeared in issue 7 of Christian History *magazine. Used by permission.*

*T*here usually is, as an old friend of Narnia ought to have remembered, more than one way in.

Doors in Oxford where C. S. Lewis passed through.

OXFORD AND C. S. LEWIS: "THE DEEPEST THIRST WITHIN US"

DEBORAH SMITH DOUGLAS

Deborah Smith Douglas, who has loved Lewis and Narnia since she was a child, is an Episcopal laywoman, a spiritual director and writer, a wife and mother. She is the author of The Praying Life: Seeking God in All Things *and, with her husband David Douglas, of* Pilgrims in the Kingdom: Travels in Christian Britain.

Historic Oxford (like the past and like life itself) is mysteriously full of doors. Even if the ones you want seem closed to you at first, keep hoping and trying: there is generally another way in.

I am on the outside, looking in. And the porter is on to me: twice now I have tried, under cover of the lawful entry of Oxford dons, to slip past the watchful old dragon and attain the sacred precincts of Magdalen College. Each time, however, he has pounced and stopped me, triumphantly reminding me what a placard has already largely declared: THE COLLEGE IS CLOSED TO ALL VISITORS.

"We are resurfacing," the porter announces importantly, although what that might mean baffles me. The tantalizing glimpses through the gateway of stone walls, grassy quad, quiet flower beds, and neat paths all reveal perfectly adequate surfaces, as far as I can see.

I explain that I have come a long way to pay homage to one of the college's most eminent fellows, C. S. Lewis, and that I merely want the most reverent, brief, and noninvasive of visits to Addison's Walk (the site of a starlit epiphany in Lewis's conversion to Christianity).

"Addison's Walk, is it?" the porter sniffs indignantly. "That's part of the Fellows' Garden, miss. You'd never be allowed in there in any event."

I have come so far and am now so near that I can hardly bear it that the way is closed to me. However, as at many other difficult moments in my life, I draw strength from recalling a passage in one of Lewis's Chronicles of Narnia.

At the beginning of *The Silver Chair*, Jill and Eustace are desperately trying to find a way out of their school grounds, away from the bullies who are chasing them. They long for the peace and freedom of the open country that lies beyond the school wall.

"If only the door was open again!" said Scrubb as they went on, and Jill nodded. For at the top of the shrubbery was a high stone wall and in that wall a door by which you could get out onto open moor. This door was nearly always locked. But there had been times when people had found it open; or perhaps there had been only one time. But you may imagine how the memory of even one time kept people hoping, and trying the door.[1]

Taking courage from the example of Jill and Eustace, I am determined to keep "hoping, and trying the door." I retreat from the college gate to rethink my approach. There must be another way in: even in Narnia, the wardrobe wasn't the only door.

The narrow Oxford streets have been noisy and crowded with the perennial tourists and flurries of newly arrived undergraduates; exhaust from enormous buses

The deer park that Jack loved at Magdalen College.

fouls the air. I am grateful for the leafy quiet of the Angel Meadow just on the other side of Magdalen Bridge. From here, on the far side of the Cherwell as it slides by, I can see into the famous, frustratingly near, Magdalen College deer park. Just beyond, I know, is Addison's Walk, where on a fateful night in the fall of 1931 Lewis strolled with his friends J. R. R. Tolkien and Hugo Dyson and somehow in the course of their conversation came finally to believe that Christianity was true.

Also on the far side of the river, beyond the barred gate, are Lewis's own suite of college rooms, the hall where he ate, the chapel where he prayed—all as inaccessible to me as if they were on the moon. I walk a long way down the riverbank, seeking a way across—a bridge, a boat, stepping-stones, anything—but finally, as the afternoon light begins to fade, so does my hope. When Jill and Eustace reached the door in the wall, it was, by the grace of Aslan, unlocked and opened into Narnia itself. But it seems I am to be shut out of Magdalen after all. Forlorn and disappointed, I acknowledge my exile.

Gradually, however, I begin to notice the wind whispering in the magnificent old horse chestnut trees that tower and branch overhead like cathedral vaulting. I remember that when Lewis recalled that momentous night's conversation, he spoke of wind in trees just like these, a stone's throw away on the other side of the Cherwell: "A rush of wind which came so suddenly on the still, warm evening and sent so many leaves pattering down that we thought it was raining. We held our breath."[2] Now I too catch my breath, remembering his memory as if it were my own, feeling the mystery of that long-past night breathe on my face. Suddenly C. S. Lewis, whose books have always fed and shaped my faith, feels near at hand, the powerful freedom of that rushing wind as close as the breath in my lungs. Perhaps the reality of that epiphany is not so remote as I had thought.

There usually is, as an old friend of Narnia ought to have remembered, more than one way in.

On the path in front of me, windfall horse chestnuts—called "conkers"—shine darkly from among the fallen leaves, and

View of Magdalen College from Addison's Walk.

Horse chestnut, or "conker," as found along Addison's Walk.

I am further comforted. "Buckeyes" we called them when I was a child, and we would gather them on autumn walks with my beloved Ohio grandmother. Impulsively I pick one up and put it in my pocket. Its smooth roundness reassures me as I close my hand around it.

The complicated sensations of that moment under the wind-murmuring trees on the banks of the river—part heart-lifting awe, part piercing sadness, memory entwined with longing and with love—Lewis himself knew well. He called it joy. It would be difficult to exaggerate the importance of this recurrent experience of joy for Lewis. In his spiritual autobiography, significantly titled *Surprised by Joy*, he claims that "in a sense the central story of my life is about nothing else."[3]

Lewis carefully distinguished joy from pleasure or happiness. Joy is a sharp desire, a mystical longing both painful and sweet, a kind of spiritual homesickness for a home we scarcely remember. Joy is, as Lewis's friend Tolkien explained it, "a sudden and miraculous grace . . . beyond the walls of the world, poignant as grief."[4] The elusive link with memory is key: the first time Lewis experienced joy was "itself the memory of a memory"—the fragrance of a flowering currant bush reminded him suddenly of a toy garden his older brother Warren had created with moss and twigs in the lid of a biscuit tin and brought into the nursery when Lewis was about four years old.[5]

Lewis eventually came to realize that his experience of joy was essentially mystical, an experience of the natural world as revelation of the goodness and love of God.

The memory of that toy garden made him "aware of nature . . . as something cool, dewy, fresh, exuberant." It was "the first beauty I ever knew," and he knew it as a message from a far country. It awakened within him a profound longing for the source of that beauty: "As long as I live my imagination of Paradise will retain something of my brother's toy garden."[6]

Joy
. . . IN A SENSE THE CENTRAL STORY OF MY LIFE IS ABOUT NOTHING ELSE.
—C. S. LEWIS, *SURPRISED BY JOY*

Warren (called Warnie) and Lewis (called Jack) remained close friends all their lives. "We were allies, not to say confederates, from the first," Lewis wrote.[7] After the death of their mother when Jack was nine, the bereft brothers came "to rely more and more exclusively on each other for all that made life bearable; to have confidence only in each other."[8] It is easy to imagine the brothers in an autumn wood like this Oxford one, companionably gathering conkers

in the time-honored schoolboy manner. With an obscure but haunting gratitude for all our childhoods—theirs, and mine, and those of all the children of Narnia—I firmly grip the conker in my pocket and turn around, to cross the bridge and head back to town.

It is dusk when I regain the High Street; the shops are closing, the college bells beginning to toll six o'clock. Remembering the summer I spent in Oxford in my own student days and the refreshment of sung evensong at Christ Church, I impulsively turn left at St. Aldate's and find a seat in the choir of the tiny, nearly empty Christ Church Cathedral.

As I kneel to pray, I notice on the narrow shelf directly in front of me, gleaming auburn in the dim light, a perfect horse chestnut. A beauty of a conker, twin to the one from the trees by the river. I accept it gratefully and tuck it with the other inside my jacket pocket.

Ironically, I was possibly closer to Lewis in that sense of exile—the painful consciousness of being excluded from some marvelous reality just on the other side of a closed door—than I might have been if the porter had allowed me the longed-for glimpse of Addison's Walk. Images of doors, gates, and magical entries abound in Lewis's writing, testimony to his own "longing to be on the inside of some door which we have always seen from the outside."[9] There is indeed perhaps no more characteristic, no more valuable, insight from Lewis's entire canon than his deep awareness that we are, all our mortal lives, far from our real home. He reminds us that we long to return, that "the deepest thirst within [us is] not adapted to the deepest nature of the world."[10] As he reasoned, "If I find in myself a desire which no experience in this world can satisfy, the most probable explanation is that I was made for another world."[11]

This "lifelong nostalgia, our longing to be reunited with something in the universe from which we now feel cut off" is, Lewis insisted, "the truest index of our real situation"[12] and in fact one of the best things about our pilgrim human state. "Our best havings are wantings," as Lewis wrote to a friend.[13] Psyche realizes in Lewis's novel *Till We Have Faces* that "the sweetest thing in all my life has been the longing to find the place where all the beauty came from."[14] These inconsolable longings are a kind of homing device, placed in our hearts by grace. Joy is sweet, even in its knife-edged sadness, because it is a gift from God, who longs, beyond all our imaginings, to draw us to himself.

Throughout the Narnia Chronicles, Lewis infuses his characters' adventures with experiences of joy. In these moments, consistent with his own experience as a child, memories of earlier times in Narnia and a yearning to return—and especially to meet Aslan again—are key. In a lyrical passage at the end of *The Lion, the Witch and the Wardrobe*, Lewis assumes his readers also have shared this piercing longing and makes a direct appeal to that memory. After many adventures, Aslan and the children finally reach the castle of Cair Paravel on its little hill by the sea:

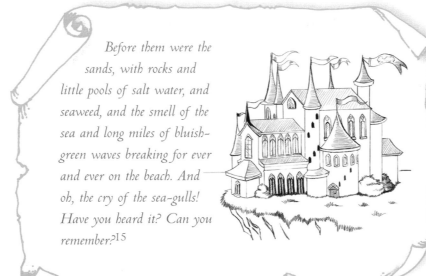

Before them were the sands, with rocks and little pools of salt water, and seaweed, and the smell of the sea and long miles of bluish-green waves breaking for ever and ever on the beach. And oh, the cry of the sea-gulls! Have you heard it? Can you remember?[15]

About three miles from the center of Oxford is the village of Headington Quarry, on the outskirts of which Jack and Warnie shared a rambling brick house, called The Kilns. Lewis also had his rooms in college, of course, where he met with students for tutorials and gathered with his friends, but the Kilns was really his home from 1930 until his death in 1963.[16]

Remembering my thwarted efforts to get into Magdalen College, I was careful not to assume that I would be allowed to enter the hallowed precincts of The Kilns, now privately owned. Nevertheless, the following morning I boarded the Headington bus, as Lewis (who never learned to drive a car) habitually did for decades.

The bus ride itself is part of the pilgrims' route: Lewis records a decisive moment in his long journey toward Christian faith that occurred on the top of a Headington bus—a moment that had everything to do with doorways into other worlds, with finally saying yes to the invitations of God.

I was going up Headington Hill on the top of a bus. . . .

I became aware that I was holding something at bay, or shutting something out. . . . I felt myself being, there and then, given a free choice. I could open the door or keep it shut. . . . I knew that to open the door . . . meant the incalculable. . . . I chose to open. . . . Enough had been thought, and said, and felt, and imagined. It was about time that something should be done.[17]

Lewis had, after long toying with philosophical and intellectual constructs of Christianity, come to the crossroads. He recognized that a "wholly new situation" had developed: "I was to be allowed to play at philosophy no longer. . . . Total surrender, the absolute leap in the dark, were demanded."[18]

Getting off the bus at Risinghurst, the stop beyond Headington Quarry, I ask my way, street by street, from young women with babies in prams and old men with garden rakes, and eventually find a small sign indicating the entrance to The Kilns. It is a handsome two-story house of mellow brick, set in lovely gardens, still ablaze with late flowers, sheltering under grand old trees.

With some trepidation I knock on the side door (neatly marked "Tradesmen's Entrance," which I doubt it was when Lewis lived there), and explain my errand to the

pleasant young Englishwoman who opens it. She is a recently qualified physician, a tenant-cum-caretaker at The Kilns, which has been purchased by an American organization to be a kind of Lewis study and conference center. Despite the early hours and despite having herself no particular interest in C. S. Lewis, she courteously offers to show me around. I am grateful for the chance to see inside the carefully "restored" house, which is far more attractive than I had imagined somehow, but the general ambiance is flat: there is no mystery (and not much reality) here.

Frankly bewildered by the extravagant reverence paid the house by her landlords, my guide points out the ceiling of the study, once stained yellow with smoke from countless Lewisian pipes: it has been carefully painted over, and then

expensively repainted to resemble a smoke-stained ceiling.

Upstairs, in the bedroom where Lewis slept for many years and where he died, I am suddenly both moved and embarrassed. I admit my own discomfort at trespassing on such intimate space. The young woman nods sympathetically. "One wonders how he would feel," she agrees. "Surely he would rather people simply read his books and left it at that."

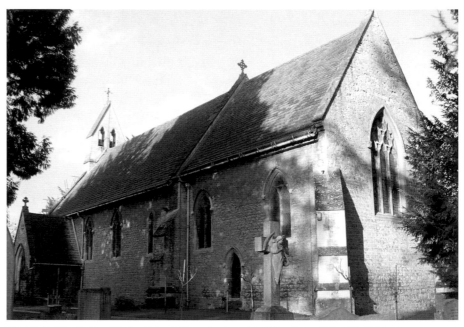

Holy Trinity Church, the parish where Jack and Warren Lewis worshipped, is a short walk from The Kilns.

Holy Trinity Church, the rural-feeling Anglican parish where Jack and Warren Lewis worshipped, is a short walk from

The Kilns, and a glorious one on this fine October morning. The Lewis brothers loved these woods, especially in autumn, with "its still, windless days . . . and all the yellow leaves still on the trees."[19] The small stone church is set in a tranquil churchyard with flagged paths winding among ancient yew trees and lichen-covered gravestones. It is difficult to believe that the noise and congestion of Oxford are so close. This place might be deep in the peaceful countryside.

Once again I encounter a locked door, but this time I am not about to be turned away. The young rector, whom I find at the rectory next door, cheerfully lends me his own key, and for an hour I am completely alone in the church. Rarely, however, has my solitude been so richly companioned.

About halfway down the side aisle on the north side, a discreet brass plaque marks the pew where the Lewis brothers sat together in church on Sunday mornings.

It is a small pew, only big enough for two, as one of the stone pillars interrupts at that point, conveniently separating the brothers from their neighbors, and sheltering them from view. I sit there myself for a long time, praying with and for them—two bulky middle-aged men in tweeds and flannels, reclusive and protective of each other.

Poignantly the window nearest the abbreviated pew is a memorial window to two other brothers, boys in the parish who died young. It would be striking anywhere. Made not of traditional stained glass but of clear glass delicately engraved, it creates shifting effects of light and shadow through which the trees and sky can be half seen. Moving closer to examine the etching, my heart lifts to recognize scenes from all of Narnia. There is Aslan himself, radiant as the sun, and the lamppost, and the valiant little *Dawn Treader*.

Left: The interior of Holy Trinity Church.
Right: A memorial window near the Lewis brothers' pew, engraved with illustrations from the Narnia Chronicles.

There is Jill riding on the back of Glimfeather the owl. There is Reepicheep, and all the talking beasts, and the trees and mountains and rivers of a country I have known and loved since I was ten. My own true country in my childhood, which I would have entered without hesitation at any moment of my life if any actual way had ever opened to me, and which in fact I inhabit still, still claim as homeland, in the imagination of my heart.

C. S. Lewis always remembered vividly the frosty October evening at a train station bookstall when he picked up a used copy of *Phantastes* by George MacDonald, a book through which "the wind of Joy" blew continuously. "That night my imagination was . . . baptized," he later realized.[20] Lewis's own Narnia Chronicles baptized mine; it was he who taught me to lift my face to those mysterious winds, to love and to seek my own true country.

Lewis spoke once (at evensong, at the Oxford University Church of St. Mary the Virgin) about joy, about the sense of exile that seems inseparable from our perception of beauty, about our "desire for our own far-off country, which we find in ourselves even now":

WE DO NOT WANT MERELY TO SEE BEAUTY . . . WE WANT . . . TO BE UNITED WITH THE BEAUTY WE SEE, TO PASS INTO IT, TO RECEIVE IT INTO OURSELVES, . . . TO BECOME PART OF IT.

Lewis went on to assure his audience that this longing will not go forever unsatisfied:

At present we are on the outside of the world, the wrong side of the door. We discern the freshness and purity of morning, but they do not make us fresh and pure. We cannot mingle with the splendours we see. But all the leaves of the New Testament are rustling with the rumour that it will not always be so. Some day, God willing, we shall get *in*.[21]

Decades before I read that lyrical promise, I had already encountered its truth in Narnia. In *The Silver Chair* (in what remains one of my favorite passages), the children, who have been held as prisoners in the dark Underworld, escape from the evil queen and begin to attempt their way out of darkness.

Finally they come to a hole high on the wall of the tunnel in which they are traveling, a hole through which shines a pale blue light. Jill climbs up and through the hole—and finds herself in Narnia again at last. She finds herself, in fact, emerging high on a moonlit hillside in the middle of a midwinter night. She is watching the Great Snow Dance, "which is done every year in Narnia on the first moonlit night when there is snow on the ground," in which a circle of dancing Fauns and Dryads is enclosed within a ring of Dwarfs circling in the opposite direction, skillfully throwing snowballs in between the dancers.

They were throwing them through the dance in such perfect time with the music and with such perfect aim that if all the dancers were in exactly the right place at exactly the right moments, no one would be hit. . . . On fine nights when the cold and the drum-taps, and the hooting of the owls, and the moonlight, have got into their wild woodland blood and made it even wilder, they will dance till daybreak. I wish you could see it for yourselves.[22]

This moment of emergence and recognition is, in its own Narnian way, a beatific vision of redemption. "They had not only got out into the Upper World at last, but had come out in the heart of Narnia. Jill felt she could have fainted with delight." Knowing that their deliverance has been accomplished, that their long captivity is over, Jill turns to shout down to the others, "I say! It's all right. We're out, and we're home."[23]

I have one more thing to do before I leave the churchyard. It does not take long to find the grave; small arrows on low signs show the way. The Lewis brothers are buried

The burial site of Jack Lewis and his brother Warren.

together under a flat granite stone (almost exactly the size and shape of a large door). The brothers' names and the dates of their lives are carved in the lower half of the stone; the upper half is occupied by a deeply incised cross. I stand at the foot of the grave for a long time, unexpectedly overwhelmed by an awareness of all I owe to Lewis, my lifelong teacher and guide. I am brimful of awe and gratitude, love and sorrow, memory and desire: a joy, in fact, as poignant as grief. I wish, suddenly, that I had thought to bring flowers; I long to make some kind of offering.

The sun is bright, making dancing shadows on the dappled ground, but the wind is cold, scattering leaves over the stone. I push

my hands into my jacket pockets and find the two conkers I put there the day before. Impulsively I bring them out to lay on the grave and, kneeling, discover that once again someone has been there before me: at the center of the cross, so deeply tucked into the space that I had not noticed it before, another perfect conker rests.

I add my two, making a burnished trinity of childish homage.

It is deeply good to know that "it's all right," that Lewis, like Jill and the others, has "got in." Thanks be to God, Jack and Warren Lewis are, as we all shall be someday, safely and forever on the far side of the door, inside at last. At home.

ENDNOTES:

1. C. S. Lewis, *The Silver Chair* (New York: The Macmillan Company, 1953), 8.
2. Humphrey Carpenter, *The Inklings: C. S. Lewis, J. R. R. Tolkien, Charles Williams, and Their Friends* (Boston: Houghton Mifflin Company, 1979), 43.
3. C. S. Lewis, *Surprised by Joy: The Shape of My Early Life* (New York: Harcourt, Brace and Company, 1956), 17.
4. J. R. R. Tolkien, "On Fairy-Stories," in *Essays Presented to Charles Williams* (Grand Rapids, Mich.: William B. Eerdmans Publishing Co., 1966), 81.
5. Lewis, *Surprised by Joy*, 16.
6. Ibid., 7.
7. Ibid., 6.
8. Ibid., 19.
9. C. S. Lewis, "The Weight of Glory" in *The Weight of Glory and Other Addresses* (Grand Rapids, Mich.: William B. Eerdmans Publishing Co., 1965), 12.
10. C. S. Lewis, *The Pilgrim's Regress: An Allegorical Apology for Christianity Reason and Romanticism* (Grand Rapids, Mich.: William B. Eerdmans Publishing Co., 1958), 148.
11. C. S. Lewis, *Mere Christianity* (New York: Macmillan Publishing Co., 1960), 120.
12. Lewis, "The Weight of Glory," 12.
13. Lewis to Dom Bede Griffiths, 5 November 1959, *Letters of C. S. Lewis*, ed. W. H. Lewis (New York: Harcourt, Brace & World, 1966), 289.
14. C. S. Lewis, *Till We Have Faces: A Myth Retold* (Grand Rapids, Mich.: William B. Eerdmans Publishing Co., 1966), 75.
15. C. S. Lewis, *The Lion, the Witch and the Wardrobe* (Harmondsworth, Middlesex, England: Penguin Books, 1959), 164.
16. The Lewis brothers also shared the house with Mrs. Janie Moore, the mother of a friend of C. S. Lewis who died in World War I. For an account of this relationship, see George Sayer, *Jack: C. S. Lewis and His Times* (San Francisco: Harper & Row, 1988).
17. Lewis, *Surprised by Joy*, 224–25.
18. Ibid., 227–28.
19. C. S. Lewis to Warren H. Lewis, 22 November 1931, unpublished letter cited in Sayer, *Jack*, 143.
20. Lewis, *Surprised by Joy*, 181.
21. Lewis, *The Weight of Glory and Other Addresses*, 12–13.
22. Lewis, *The Silver Chair*, 193.
23. Ibid., 192.

The pursuit of knowledge.

Dr. Cornelius

Lewis served as a Fellow at Magdalen College, where he pursued things of the mind with fervor.
One of Lewis's characters from the Narnia Chronicles, Dr. Cornelius, embodied this spirit of scholarship.

❦3❧

THE INKLINGS . . . AND OTHER INFLUENCES

Magdalen College: Lewis's room was on the second floor, near the middle.

The Eagle and Child pub, also known by Jack as the Bird and Baby.

Without doubt, Lewis's creative and theological genius was stimulated by his weekly meetings with the "Inklings," a collection of thinkers and friends who gathered regularly to critique one another's writing and to discuss current events and life in general. The name of the group was transferred from an Oxford literary society in which Lewis and J. R. R. Tolkien had been members to a group of friends who gathered in Lewis's rooms at Magdalen College every Thursday night.

Usually present were C. S. Lewis, Warren Lewis, J. R. R. Tolkien, Dr. R. E. Havard, and Charles Williams. Other attendees included Nevill Coghill, Hugo Dyson, Owen Barfield, and Adam Fox.

A focus of the meetings was the reading aloud of works in progress for criticism. Inklings heard and discussed first drafts of Tolkien's *Lord of the Rings*, Lewis's *The Great Divorce*, and Warren Lewis's book on Louis XIV. In addition, they read and critiqued their own poetry and that of others. Lively discussions ensued on such topics as education, pain, horror comics, and who was the most important man in various countries. Much disagreement is reported to have occurred, and members sometimes expressed intense dislike for one another's work.

The Inklings began meeting in Lewis's rooms around 1933 and continued that Thursday evening tradition until 1950. Tuesday morning gatherings at the Eagle and Child public house (known as the Bird and Baby) continued until Lewis's death.

A gallery of thumbnail sketches of close and influential family and friends of C. S. Lewis:

Albert Lewis

suited him for a career in politics if he had had the means. Albert's favorite pastime was spending an afternoon swapping anecdotes with his brothers, acting them out with great flourish.

C. S. Lewis described his father's side of the family as "true Welshmen, sentimental, passionate, and rhetorical, easily moved both to anger and to tenderness." Albert never fully recovered from grief following his wife's death, and his erratic and sometimes cruel subsequent behavior alienated his sons.

Albert filled the Lewis home with books, but his son's interest in fantasy literature was not shared by his parents. "If I am a romantic," he wrote, "my parents bear no responsibility for it."

she agreed to marry Albert after an eight-year courtship, she wrote to him, "I wonder do I love you? I am not quite sure. I know that at least I am very fond of you, and that I should never think of loving anyone else."

C. S. Lewis wrote of her family, "Their minds were critical and ironic, and they had the talent for happiness to a high degree." Flora was a voracious reader and wrote magazine articles. She died of cancer when C. S. Lewis was nine. "With my mother's death," he wrote, "all that was tranquil and reliable disappeared from my life."

Florence Hamilton Lewis

ALBERT LEWIS (1863–1929)

C. S. Lewis's father, Albert Lewis, was the son of a Welsh immigrant who found success as a partner in a firm that manufactured boilers and ships. Albert attended college and began a practice as a solicitor in Belfast in 1885.

Lewis believed his father's quick mind, eloquence, and love of oratory would have

FLORENCE HAMILTON LEWIS (1862–1908)

Flora Lewis, C. S. Lewis's mother, was the daughter of the Rev. Thomas Hamilton, rector of the church attended by the Lewises. Flora's talent for mathematics won her a first in the subject at Queen's College, Belfast, where she earned a B.A.

Flora's cool temperament was the antithesis of her husband's emotionality. When

Major Warren Hamilton Lewis
(1895–1973)

C. S. Lewis referred to his older brother, Warren ("Warnie"), as "my dearest and closest friend." The lifelong bond formed as the boys played together, writing and illustrating stories, in their country home. When their mother's death devastated their father, they were left with only each other for comfort and support.

Although their careers took widely different turns, the two lived together much of their lives. Warren was a career army officer in the Royal Army Service Corps and served in such posts as Sierra Leone and China. After retiring from eighteen years of active service in 1932, he took up residence at The Kilns, where he lived until after his brother's death.

Upon retirement, Warren took on the task of editing the Lewis family papers. He was recalled to active service in World War II. During his final retirement he wrote seven books on the history of seventeenth-century France.

Warren Lewis returned to belief in Christianity five months before his brother's conversion. He was a frequent participant in weekly meetings of the Inklings. The Lewis brothers undertook many annual walking tours of up to fifty miles. His forty-year battle with alcoholism was a source of great concern to his brother.

Jack and Warren Lewis.

was also a consistent influence for Christ in his friend's life, and it was to Greeves that Lewis first revealed his own conversion.

Greeves's heart ailment prevented him from holding steady employment. Independently wealthy, he never needed it. He earned a certificate of art at a London school and was considered a good painter. Although he also wrote, Greeves was never published. Lewis sent Greeves some of his manuscripts for critique.

Arthur Greeves

ARTHUR GREEVES
(1895–1966)

C. S. Lewis described Arthur Greeves as "after my brother, my oldest and most intimate friend." Lewis met Greeves when the neighbor boy, bedridden with a bad heart that kept him an invalid most of his life, requested a visit. The two boys discovered a common love for books, and Lewis found in Greeves an "alter ego, the many who first reveals to you that you are not alone in the world by turning out (beyond hope) to share all your most secret delights."

Although Lewis did not consider Greeves his intellectual equal, he learned much from Greeves's insight into the realm of feelings. The two began a correspondence that lasted for the rest of Lewis's life, and he wrote his friend nearly three hundred letters. Greeves

Owen Barfield

OWEN BARFIELD
(1898–1997)

C. S. Lewis and Owen Barfield were drawn together during their undergraduate days at Oxford by a common interest in poetry. As they read and critiqued each other's work, Lewis found in Barfield a second great friend. The two men shared interests but not

points of view; Lewis described Barfield as his "anti-self," "the man who disagrees with you about everything."

After Oxford, Barfield worked as a freelance writer until financial demands forced him to enter his father's legal firm as a solicitor. He maintained his friendship with Lewis for the rest of their lives and was influential in shaping Lewis's views about the importance of myth in language, literature, and the history of thinking. Barfield resumed his writing career after retiring from law.

Raised an agnostic, Barfield became a Christian in his late twenties; nevertheless, he was never comfortable with Lewis's apologetics or his evangelism. He later embraced and wrote about anthroposophy, a form of religious philosophy which he believed complemented rather than detracted from Christianity.

J. R. R. TOLKIEN
(1892–1973)

Although they initially took opposite sides in a faculty dispute over English literature curriculum, Tolkien and Lewis were eventually united by an interest in myth and legend. Tolkien introduced Lewis to the Coalbiters, a club he had formed which read and translated Icelandic myths. Their mutual interest led to many late-night discussions and long walks. Lewis wrote to Greeves that

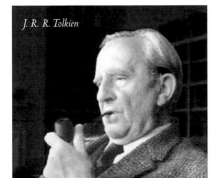
J. R. R. Tolkien

Tolkien was "the one man absolutely fitted, if fate had allowed, to be a third in our friendship in the old days."

Their shared belief in the importance of myth led to a discussion about Christianity that Lewis regarded an important factor leading to his conversion. Lewis encouraged Tolkien in his work on *The Silmarillion*, a cycle of myth and legend, and read *The Lord of the Rings* as Tolkien wrote it. Tolkien was extremely critical of Lewis's Narnian chronicles, charging that they were hastily written, inconsistent, and that they failed to create a "real" setting. Tolkien was also critical of Lewis's marriage to Joy, party because of his views on divorce and remarriage.

Tolkien was professor of Anglo-Saxon at Oxford from 1925 to 1945, when he became professor of English language and literature until retirement in 1959.

CHARLES WILLIAMS
(1886–1945)

The son of a clerk who instilled in him his love of literature and belief in understanding all sides of an argument, Charles Williams was largely self-educated. Williams began his career as a proofreader in the London office of Oxford University Press, where he worked his way up to the position of editor. Williams wrote poetry from his early days and became a prolific writer of novels, drama, theology, and criticism as well.

Charles Williams

Williams met Lewis when the latter wrote him a letter praising his novel *The Place of the Lion*. At the same time, Williams was admiring Lewis's *Allegory of Love*. The two met occasionally until Williams moved to Oxford in 1939, where he became a regular member of the Inklings.

Although Lewis described Williams as "ugly as a chimpanzee," Williams's personal magnetism won him a wide following. He developed the idea of romantic theology, which considers the theological implications of romantic experiences, and *The Way of Affirmation*, in which earthly pleasures are seen as a door to Christian vision rather than a barrier.

Lewis was impressed by Williams's selfless character and described him as offering himself wholly to others without expecting anything in return. Although Lewis said he was never consciously influenced by Williams's work, many students of the two see Williams's influence in Lewis's writing, especially in using ordinary people as the characters in the Space Trilogy.

DOROTHY SAYERS
(1893–1957)

Dorothy Sayers, one of the first female graduates of Oxford, studied the classics and won honors in modern language studies. She worked as an advertising copywriter for eleven years. Sayers first won recognition as the writer of detective thrillers featuring Lord Peter Wimsey. She later wrote religious plays for radio as well as numerous books and essays on Christian apologetics and theology.

Dorothy Sayers

Sayers kept up correspondence, primarily concerning literature, with Lewis and his contemporaries. Lewis considered her "the first person of importance who ever wrote me a fan letter," and he called her "one of the great English letter writers." It may have been Sayers who spurred Lewis to write *Miracles*; he began work on the book just weeks after receiving her letter lamenting no good modern works on the subject.

Sayers was a member of Oxford's Socratic Club, a forum for discussing intellectual challenges in religion and Christianity, of which Lewis was president for twenty-two years. Lewis appreciated Sayers in person as well as by post; he praised "the extraordinary zest and edge of her conversation."

JOY DAVIDMAN
(1915–1960)

Helen Joy Davidman, of Jewish decent, was raised in the Bronx, New York, where she readily adopted her father's materialistic philosophy. Extraordinarily bright, she entered college at fourteen. By the age of twenty-five, she had earned a master's degree and published a novel and two books of poetry. After a failed try at screenwriting in Hollywood, she settled in New York to continue her work with the Communist Party. There she met and married William Gresham, a fellow writer.

Joy Davidman

Joy found faith in God in her early thirties and became a Christian a year later, partly through the influence of Lewis's

books. She began correspondence with him that led to a visit and a growing friendship. When her husband left her for another woman, she moved to Oxford with her two sons.

Lewis described Joy's mind as "lithe and quick and muscular as a leopard." Many of his friends disapproved of the match; some found Joy too harsh and outspoken; others objected to her status as a divorcee. Nevertheless, their brief marriage, which ended in her death from cancer, brought some of the greatest joy to his life. Joy encouraged Lewis to write *Reflections on the Psalms*, and her influence can be seen in *Till We Have Faces* and *The Four Loves*. Her own book, *Smoke on the Mountain*, is still in print.

G. K. CHESTERTON
(1874–1936)

One of Lewis's primary mentors in apologetics, and an influence even in his conversion, was G. K. Chesterton. Novelist, poet, essayist, and journalist, Chesterton was perhaps best known for his Father Brown detective stories. He produced more than one hundred volumes in his lifetime, including biographies on St. Francis of Assisi and St. Thomas Aquinas. His *The Everlasting Man*,

G. K. Chesterton

which set out a Christian outline of history, was one of the factors that wore down Lewis's resistance to Christianity.

Chesterton was one of the first defenders of orthodoxy to use humor as a weapon. Perhaps more important was his use of reason to defend faith. Chesterton wrote that the universe can only be understood as a creation; that man's sense of right and wrong and his conflict when he becomes aware that he is not what he was made to be points to a Creator. Though they never met, Lewis called Chesterton "the most sensible man alive."

GEORGE MACDONALD
(1824–1905)

The man C. S. Lewis regarded as his master barely made a living as a poet, novelist, lecturer, and writer of children's books. Yet as Lewis said of the retired minister, "I know hardly any other writer who seems to be closer, or more continually close, to the Spirit of Christ Himself." In his teens Lewis was profoundly changed by reading MacDonald's *Phantastes: A Faerie Romance,* an experience Lewis considered the "baptism" of his imagination. Lewis considered MacDonald the best writer of fantasy alive, and he found a sense of holiness in all MacDonald's writings. Lewis was touched by MacDonald's devotional writings as well. He wrote, "My own debt to *[Unspoken Sermons]* is almost as great as one man can owe to another," and he recommended the book with success to many seekers.

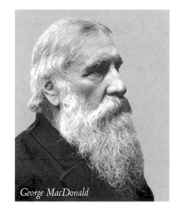

George MacDonald

Source: This article first appeared in issue 7 of *Christian History* magazine. Used by permission.

*T*he children feel so close to Aslan. —WALTER HOOPER

The Kilns.

4

FRIENDS OF LEWIS, FRIENDS OF OLD NARNIA

JAMES S. C. BAEHR

Do you take sugar with that? Walter Hooper, C. S. Lewis's personal secretary and friend, is sitting in front of a pot of tea at his home in North Oxford. Images from the classical past adorn this place; Greek and Roman statues and busts stare down at us from every corner. It reminds me a little of the witch's statuary. I almost expect these forms to come to life as we speak of the Lion. This place, of course, is filled only with friends of Old Narnia—Walter, myself, and his wise and precocious cat, Claret the Meek.

"Lewis took four spoonfuls of sugar with every cup of tea," Walter remembers. "Four spoonfuls." He shakes his head jovially at the excess.

"The first time I met Lewis was on the tenth of June in 1963." Walter begins recounting his memories of Lewis confidently, as our conversation commences. He speaks in an accent influenced both by his native North Carolina and this British nation.

"I came to look for his house a few days early because it was well hidden and I didn't want to miss it on the day of our appointment. I couldn't find it. One woman finally told me how to find it and suggested I just head over then and introduce myself. It was about four o'clock."

Walter took the woman up on her suggestion and was pleasantly surprised.

"He couldn't be nicer. How kind he was. We sat and talked for hours."

Lewis soon proved himself both friendly and playful.

"I went through three cups of tea and was about to burst. So I asked Lewis if I could use the bathroom. Lewis said, 'Of course,' and took me through the house to the bath.

He took out towels and soap and everything and asked, 'Do you have enough for a bath?' I said yes. After he had left, I went back out and admitted that I needed to use the toilet, not take a bath. Lewis burst out laughing. 'Oh, I knew that! That will cure you of your American expressions!'"

The meeting went so well, Hooper almost regretted it:

"As our time together drew to a close, I realized I liked him so much. Maybe it would have been better to not have met him at all."

Of course, Lewis would have none of this. Not only did he invite Hooper to the Inklings meeting; he later asked him if he would be able to serve as his personal secretary. Lewis's brother, Warnie, typically fulfilled that role, but his struggles with alcohol left him frequently absent and extremely unreliable. Hooper worked as Lewis's aide on and off until his death. While Lewis had written the Narnia series in the previous decade, he and Hooper discussed many of his works.

"I found he didn't bring up his books," said Walter, "He was a very modest man. When we talked about them, he would talk as just someone who also happened to like them, not as their author."

Hooper remembers some of Lewis's character inspirations, though.

"Lewis had a gardener named Paxford who was a model for Puddleglum. He mostly talked about Paxford's contribution to it. I think Puddleglum may be the most imaginative of Lewis's creations."

Puddleglum, of course, is the marsh-wiggle found in *The Silver Chair*. Puddleglum proves a difficult figure to place.

LEWIS'S GARDENER
PAXFORD
SERVED AS A
MODEL FOR
𝔓UDDLEGLUM.

On the one hand, he proves excessively dour, constantly pointing out the worst possible take on the situation at hand. On the other, his heroic faith and personal sacrifice save the children at their moments of greatest need. Walter goes on about Paxford: "Lewis loved fresh vegetables. One day, we were looking through the garden shed window and saw on the table a beautiful, red, ripe tomato. We couldn't get the door open, though. It was locked. So while we were watching the tomato, it fell from the ledge and spattered right in front of us. At that moment, Paxford comes by and sees us." Walter adds a British texture to his voice as he mimics Paxford's response: "'Well, Mr. Jack, good thing I locked that door. If I hadn't locked that door you would have gotten in there while that tomato was still green and eaten it. Good thing that door was locked.'"

Lewis had wanted to take Joy to Greece before she died, Walter told me. Right before their flight, Paxford had been listening to the radio, as he always did. He came up to them to tell them about some breaking news: there had just been a gruesome airplane crash. "Burnt beyond recognition," Paxford solemnly intoned to them directly before they set off for the airport. "Burnt beyond recognition," he grimly repeated. The trip turned out to be a success, but imagining the morbid thoughts going through the group's mind as they departed made Walter and me laugh.

"It worked out tremendously well. She came back in a 'nunc dimitis' frame of mind," said Walter.

Lewis also received letters from children the world over on his Narnian series. For at least thirty-five years after Lewis's death, children were writing to the author to share thoughts and appreciation for his Narnia series. "One boy wrote Lewis to tell him, 'You're ruining my life. I used to watch TV everyday, but now that I started reading Narnia, I can't put them down. I have to read them all. It's taking up all my time. You're ruining my life.'" Hooper dismisses modern educators who say the books shouldn't be read because they would frighten children. Of all the children's letters he has read, Hooper has never found one where a child wrote in about nightmares. "The children feel so close to Aslan."

Indeed Hooper thinks Aslan is Lewis's greatest creation. "Lewis's greatest contribution to literature or writing was to say this is the Son of God in another form, and no one has ever said it doesn't sound like the Son of God."

LEWIS'S GREATEST CONTRIBUTION TO LITERATURE OR WRITING WAS TO SAY THIS IS THE SON OF GOD IN ANOTHER FORM, AND NO ONE HAS EVER SAID IT DOESN'T SOUND LIKE THE SON OF GOD.

—WALTER HOOPER

*T*he one aim of those who practice philosophy in the proper manner is to practice for dying and death. —PLATO, PHAEDO

The gravesite of C. S. Lewis.

❧5❧

WILL WE MEET PLATO IN HEAVEN?

CAROLYN STANFORD GOSS AND JOSEPH STANFORD GOSS

Carolyn Stanford Goss teaches seminars on C. S. Lewis at Williamson Christian College near Nashville, Tennessee. She earned degrees from Arizona State University and Vanderbilt University. Joseph Stanford Goss teaches philosophy and humanities at Valparaiso University in Valparaiso, Indiana. He holds degrees from the University of Michigan and Loyola University-Chicago and is the assistant editor of *The Owl of Minerva*, the journal of the Hegel Society of America.

If those who are called philosophers, especially the Platonists, have said things which are indeed true and are well accommodated to our faith, they should not be feared; rather, what they have said should be taken from them as from unjust possessors and converted to our use. Just as the Egyptians had not only idols and grave burdens which the people of Israel detested and avoided, so also they had vases and ornaments of gold and silver and clothing which the Israelites took with them secretly when they fled, as if to put them to a better use. They did not do this on their own authority but at God's commandment, while the Egyptians unwittingly supplied them with things which they themselves did not use well.

St. Augustine, *On Christian Doctrine*[1]

Is Plato in heaven? What a question! We might find ourselves quickly turning to John 14:6 and using it as a proof text for an answer in the negative: "I am the way, the truth, and the life. No one comes to the Father except through Me." In *The Silver Chair*, the fourth of The Chronicles of Narnia, Aslan similarly tells Jill Pole, who is "dying of thirst," that there is "no other stream" to drink from but the one in Aslan's path.

Yet some Christians have found themselves uncomfortable with the idea that there are those of us whom God has been so selective as to circumscribe a perimeter around. Are only those people who have been blessed or predestined or fortunate or lucky or predisposed by the good fortune of having been born into Christian-era history to have the joy of meeting the incarnate God of *all* human history? At the same time Christians find themselves bristling at the suggestion that a person who was not acquainted with the Christ they know just might be a fellow sharer in the glories of the heavenly kingdom. Jesus' words are clear.

Does it lessen our discomfort to say, at least, that Plato is like the virtuous pagans in Dante's *Inferno*? Perhaps not in torment but still forever out of sight of God and the saints? Can we go further to concede that Plato might be able to *glimpse* the golden mane? Given C. S. Lewis's own self-professed paganism both in his earlier spiritual life and in his choice of a mythological framework to convey theological truths, how might he answer this question: Is Plato in heaven? Many of us who recognize Plato's greatness and even proclaim some allegiance to him would no doubt want to meet him on the blessed isles, if we could. Our situation is similar to the one Socrates describes in the *Apology*: death might just be a great opportunity to converse with some interesting people!

C. S. Lewis was not the first, nor will he be the last, of the line of Christians who believe that Plato's thought lies at the foundation of Western philosophy and spirituality. For example, Terry Meithe's essay "Plato's Metaphysics: His Contribution to a Philosophy of God," reminds us that Alfred North Whitehead insisted that the European philosophical tradition is merely a series of footnotes to Plato (from *Taking Every Thought Captive: Essays in Honor of James D. Strauss*).[2] In fact, a stream of neo-Platonism runs through the Narnia Chronicles as the Great River runs through Narnia itself—like the Great River, created by Aslan on the very first day of Narnia's existence, Platonism is so basic to the landscape of the Chronicles that the books would not be the same without it.

The question we ask, then, is not just related to how Lewis interpreted and redirected the stream of Platonic thought but whether he might take the leap into the waters to suggest that Plato pointed the way to the Way, and that Plato's righteous paganism might be enough to usher him into the realm of the blessed. We'll suggest a possible

A STREAM OF NEO-PLATONISM RUNS THROUGH THE NARNIA CHRONICLES AS THE GREAT RIVER RUNS THROUGH NARNIA ITSELF—LIKE THE GREAT RIVER, CREATED BY ASLAN ON THE VERY FIRST DAY OF NARNIA'S EXISTENCE, PLATONISM IS SO BASIC TO THE LANDSCAPE OF THE CHRONICLES THAT THE BOOKS WOULD NOT BE THE SAME WITHOUT IT.

answer after first taking a look at two platonic thought streams that flow throughout *The Lion, the Witch and the Wardrobe* and *The Last Battle*, the first and the last books in The Chronicles of Narnia.

One important point to make at the outset is that Plato was not (and *could not have been*) a Christian. Besides the obvious historical fact that he lived some four centuries before Christ, some of his ideas do not gel with Christianity. He is an elitist, for one

thing: Plato does not believe that everyone has the same capacity to encounter ultimate reality and goodness; the idea of grace is mostly absent from Plato's work. Plato also seems to believe that human souls are not only immortal but they preexist their incarnation and are eventually reincarnated after death in a complicated, somewhat karmic, sort of system (see the *Meno* and especially the *Phaedo*). For Christians there are also other difficulties in Plato's thought—for example, in his cosmology, which describes a world creator that looks to preexisting forms for guidance in how the world is created (see the *Timaeus*). In spite of all this, Lewis redirects at least two ideas from Plato into the Christian stream of thought: the theory of forms, with its emphasis on the doctrine that there are two worlds, the real (ideal) world and the apparent world, and the necessity of moral formation and insight as preparation for death.

Let us consider first the supposition that there is a hierarchy of reality. Both Plato and Lewis maintain that there is a world that we humans experience and a different, truly "real" world that is rarely available (though not quite unavailable) in human experience, at least in the span of a normal human life. Plato teaches of an unchangeable entity called a *form* (from the Greek *eidon*, sometimes translated as "idea") that corresponds with changeable entities in the world of appearances—the sensible world in which we all live. Plato identifies forms of physical things (such as tables or beds) and forms of the attributes that attach to these things (beauty, justice, piety, and so on). There even seems to be one form, "the good," which is in its own class "beyond being" (see *Republic* 509b) in a sort of godlike supremacy over everything else.[3] The forms have a causal relation to sensible things, and Plato describes the latter as "participating" in those forms. The upshot of all this is that the world we commonly perceive is not the real world. It is instead a world of instability, where "all is flux," which points to things higher than itself as both its source and sustenance.

The second area in which Plato and Lewis seem to agree is on the necessity for consciously living a moral life, though they differ somewhat as to what the moral life is. For Lewis, the highest moral law is the divine love that enables a person to love without any direct personal benefit. We must first come to a moment of moral insight in which we not only recognize our own need for love but we also accept that need with delight. Grace then steps in, enabling us to give gift-love without expecting anything in return.[4]

For Plato the moral life can be described in a number of ways. To slightly rephrase Socrates's words from Plato's *Apology*, the moral life is the examined life: "The unexamined life is not worth living" (38a). This is a view that Plato could never be accused of abandoning—the right way to live is to live in pursuit of wisdom (*philosophy* itself means "love of wisdom"). Everything else depends on this. The experience and knowledge of justice, virtue, beauty, courage, self-control, and of course, goodness are possible only in living the examined life. Political stability depends on it, too, as revealed in the *Republic*, where the philosophers are the rulers of the city. The practice of philosophy is demanded by conscience, and Plato even equates it in the *Apology* with service to the divine. Plato also describes the practice of philosophy, the pursuit of wisdom, as preparation for death.[5] Philosophy seeks release from the things of this world, including all the body's needs and desires, and desires what is permanently abiding and stable: the forms. Upon one's physical death the soul may come into contact with ultimate reality, which is possible only temporarily in an embodied state and only for the truly disciplined.

The nature and hierarchy of reality is a major theme in *The Lion, the Witch and the Wardrobe* and *The Last Battle*. In both books Professor Kirke/Lord Digory (we have found out in earlier books that the fifty-two-year-old bachelor is the same person as Digory, the boy who was present at the creation of Narnia) knocks down the children's *a priori* assumptions about the nature of reality. In *The Lion, the Witch and the Wardrobe*, Peter, Susan, and Edmund Pevensie ask the professor's advice when Lucy keeps insisting on the reality of Narnia. The professor exclaims: "Logic! Why don't they teach logic at these schools?"

Logic! Why don't they teach logic at these schools?

—Prof. Kirk

He then points out that Lucy is more than likely talking about *another* sort of reality and discounts the children's belief that time is the same in this world and in Narnia. His reasoning causes them to admit that there may be another world besides our own.

Moreover the Pevensie children seem to have what Plato might call an innate knowledge (or recollection, *anamnesis*—see *Meno* and *Phaedo*) of forms. When they first hear the name of Aslan, none of them knows who he is, but immediately everyone feels "quite different." Lewis speculates, "Perhaps it has sometimes happened to you in a dream that someone says something which you don't understand but in the dream it feels as if it had some enormous meaning. . . . It was like that now. At the name of Aslan

each one of the children felt something jump in his inside." The two daughters of Eve and two sons of Adam seem to know that Aslan is more than just a lion in the narrow and particular sense. Rather, he embodies some quality or qualities that are fundamental, even definitive, of the concept of *lion*: "When they tried to look at Aslan's face they just caught a glimpse of the golden mane and the great, royal, solemn, overwhelming eyes; and then they found they couldn't look at him and went all trembly." His essence inspires both their awe and their worship. Aslan is the form of a lion in all its richness of meaning, and of course, to a Christian, he embodies the characteristics of the Form of forms—the Lion of Judah.

The Last Battle continues the concentration on the nature of ultimate reality. When Aslan raises Father Time to draw Narnia's days of existence to a close, he creates a new Narnia, in which all created things are so hyperreal that they are indescribable. Lewis tells us that the fruit in the new land is so delicious, so juicy, that we the readers "can't find out what it is like unless you get to that country and taste for yourself." The fruit is the apex, the model, for the finite concept of *fruit*. Digory/Kirke says that all things in the new land are "more like the real thing." According to him, the old world was only "a shadow or copy" of the real Narnia. "It's all in Plato, all in Plato. What do they teach them in these schools?" he asks. We smile when we read the Greek philosopher's

AT THE NAME OF **ASLAN** EACH ONE OF THE CHILDREN FELT SOMETHING JUMP IN HIS INSIDE.—C. S. LEWIS, *THE LION, THE WITCH AND THE WARDROBE*

name, but our initial question remains. If Plato's works contain the answers, will the *formulator*—and we use that word with great care—of them see God face-to-face along with us?

The Last Battle, the culmination of The Chronicles of Narnia, offers some possible answers to our question, as it borrows, not for the first time in The Chronicles, from Plato's Allegory of the Cave to teach some lessons about spiritual perception.[6] Diggle and his coterie of dwarfs adopt the battle cry of "The Dwarfs are for the Dwarfs!" Totally self-absorbed, they eventually end up inside the stable, where all is light and beauty, but their skewed interpretation of their surroundings keeps them in the dark. They sit in a tight, sullen group and seem to want to be in darkness and foulness rather than light. Lucy gives Diggle a bouquet of violets, and he thinks it is a handful of stable litter. Aslan shakes down a feast for the dwarfs from his mane, and they insist that it is comprised only of hay and rotten food, to be washed down with dirty trough water. Tirian tries to drag Diggle out of the blackness, only to see Diggle dart back down into the dark. John 3:19 comes to mind: "This, then, is the judgment: the light has come into the world, and people loved darkness rather than the light because their deeds were evil." The dwarfs' perception that all is darkness and their stubborn insistence on remaining in the dark remind us of the inhabitants of Plato's cave, who, from birth, see only shadows and mistakenly think the shadows are reality. They reject the insights of their former companion who comes back into the cave and tells them of the outside world. Recasting the allegory into Christian framework, Lewis also offers a profound example about spiritual perception—or the lack of it, in the dwarfs' case—and its connection to forgiveness, which, sadly, the dwarfs do not come out of their state of darkness long enough to accept.

Becoming aware of one's sinfulness (for Plato, one's ignorance) equates with insight, for Lewis. Edmund Pevensie in *The Lion, the Witch and the Wardrobe* thinks at first only of his tummy and is swept under the white witch's spell as she offers him Turkish delight. He gorges on the candy until he begins to feel more than a bit uncomfortable. Back at the professor's house, he allows Peter and Susan to assume that Lucy is telling lies about Narnia, or worse, that she is insane. Returning to the white witch, he continues to think only of his own physical needs. The moment of insight comes when the witch forces him to ride in her sledge as she pursues Aslan. She turns a merry little party of squirrels, satyrs, and other creatures who are celebrating the arrival of Father Christmas into stone. "And Edmund for the first time in this story [feels] sorry for someone besides himself." Edmund's cave has been a spiritual one, but he begins to break free of its bondage. He does not have to do anything to earn Aslan's forgiveness, but his stepping outside of his selfishness prepares his heart and mind for being able to say, "I'm sorry," first to Aslan and then to Peter, Susan, and Lucy.

EDMUND FOR THE FIRST TIME IN THIS STORY FEELS SORRY FOR SOMEONE BESIDES HIMSELF. —*THE LION, THE WITCH AND THE WARDROBE*

In *The Last Battle* we encounter another character who comes to a point of awareness that prepares him for meeting Aslan, and his portrayal provides further clues to the answer to our original question. Emeth the Calormene is an honorable man. The children observe him when he asks to go into the stable where his deity Tash allegedly resides: "He was young and tall and slender, and even rather beautiful in the dark, haughty, Calormene way," they note. In his 1980 book *Companion to Narnia*, Paul F. Ford explains that *Emeth* is from the Hebrew words for "faithful" and "true." Yet his faith is the equivalent of paganism—it's religious but is not directed at the proper object. However, when Emeth realizes that Tash is not real and he finally meets Aslan, the golden-maned lion says to him, "Child, all the service thou hast done to Tash, I account a service done to me." Later Emeth describes his encounter with Aslan. Aslan had told Emeth that "I take to me the services which thou hast done to him [Tash], for I and he are of such different kinds that no service which is vile can be done to me, and none which is not vile can be done to him." So what do these pronouncements suggest?

Taking a short tour away from The Chronicles of Narnia, let's consider Lewis's imaginative supposal of a different sort,

TASH

I TAKE TO ME THE SERVICES WHICH THOU HAST DONE TO HIM [TASH], FOR I AND HE ARE OF SUCH DIFFERENT KINDS THAT NO SERVICE WHICH IS VILE CAN BE DONE TO ME, AND NONE WHICH IS NOT VILE CAN BE DONE TO HIM.—ASLAN

The Screwtape Letters. In this satirical epistolary account, Screwtape, Undersecretary for the Infernal Lowerarchy, teaches his nephew, Wormwood, about the steps to use in the temptation of a new Christian. Lewis offers two tantalizing clues that shed light not only on his portrayal of Emeth but on Lewis's possible position regarding Plato's proposed seat at the heavenly banquet table. Screwtape tells Wormwood derisively that God "often makes prizes of humans who have given their lives for causes He thinks bad on the monstrously sophistical ground that the humans thought them good and were following the best they knew."[7] (chapter 5) It is true that Screwtape is an author of lies, but the demon often utters truth without realizing it. Could Aslan's comforting words to Emeth be an expression of a similar point of view? Screwtape also tells Wormwood that when demons "make the Sophists, He [God] raises up a Socrates to answer them." The implication of this statement seems apparent. God's purposeful creation surely has a place in heaven, doesn't it?

Perhaps so. Lewis comments that he came to realize near the end of his atheism that for Plato, philosophy wasn't just a subject, "it was a way."[8] Not *the* Way, but as Professor Kirke says, the truth is "all in Plato, all in Plato." Lewis also reveals that "I should be very sorry not to have passed through that experience. I think it is more religious than many experiences that have been called Christian. What I learned from the Idealists (and most still strongly hold) is this maxim: It is more important that Heaven should exist than that any of us should reach it."[9] Plato perhaps would agree. Plato engaged in a search for truth that Lewis's own path followed in some ways. Without realizing what his philosophy would contribute to, Plato developed ideas that would help Christians such as Lewis understand God.

"Can you by searching find out God?" Job 11:7 asks (KJV, author paraphrase). Plato didn't find the whole truth, but he made an honest attempt. "The universe rings true wherever you fairly test it," comments Lewis.[10] If a philosophical system goes only so far but not the whole way, as Lewis (and Augustine, and many other Christians sympathetic to Plato) would agree, that does not mean it is not true. It's all in Plato, all in Plato—including the possibility that both Jack Lewis and Plato will meet us at the door to the home of the Eternal Author of Forms.

God "*often makes prizes of humans who have given their lives for causes He thinks bad on the monstrously sophistical ground that the humans thought them good and were following the best they knew.*"
—C. S. Lewis,
The Screwtape Letters

Endnotes:

1. St. Augustine, *On Christian Doctrine*, book II, chapter 40, translated by D. W. Robertson Jr. (New York: Macmillan, 1958), 75.
2. Richard A. Knopp and John D. Castelein, eds., *Taking Every Thought Captive: Essays in Honor of James D. Strauss* (Joplin, Mo.: College Press, 1997), 274.
3. The form of the good becomes an important element in the neoplatonic systems of Plotinus, Porphyry, and others and reaches Christian theology in the works of (for example) Marius Victorinus, St. Augustine, and Pseudo-Dionysius.
4. C. S. Lewis, *The Four Loves* (New York: Harvest Books, 1971), 130–40.
5. *Phaedo* 64a: "The one aim of those who practice philosophy in the proper manner is to practice for dying and death" (Grube translation).
6. The Allegory of the Cave is from *Republic*, Book VII.
7. C. S. Lewis, *The Screwtape Letters* (New York: Simon & Schuster, 1996), chapter 5.
8. C. S. Lewis, *Surprised by Joy: The Shape of My Early Life* (New York: Harcourt Brace & Company, 1955), 218.
9. Ibid., 204.
10. Ibid., 171.

I do believe that God is the Father of lights—natural lights as well as spiritual lights.
—C. S. Lewis, during interview with Sherwood Wirt

6

LEWIS'S LAST INTERVIEW

MAY 7, 1963

SHERWOOD WIRT

Sherwood Eliot Wirt earned the Ph.D. degree from the University of Edinburgh and has enjoyed a long literary career that has included stints with the *San Francisco Examiner* and the *Juneau* (Alaska) *Daily Press*, where for four years he served as city editor. He has also written more than twenty-five books and edited numerous others, winning various awards for his work. This interview was adapted from one originally published in *Decision Magazine* in 1963 in two installments. Sherwood was editor of *Decision Magazine*. This article is used by permission.

WHAT IS YOUR OPINION OF THE KIND OF WRITING BEING DONE WITHIN THE CHRISTIAN CHURCH TODAY?

A great deal of what is being published by writers in the religious tradition is a scandal and is actually turning people away from the church. The liberal writers who are continually accommodating and whittling down the truth of the gospel are responsible. I cannot understand how a man can appear in print claiming to disbelieve everything that he presupposes when he puts on the surplice. I feel it is a form of prostitution.

WOULD YOU SAY THAT THE AIM OF CHRISTIAN WRITING, INCLUDING YOUR OWN WRITING, IS TO BRING ABOUT AN ENCOUNTER OF THE READER WITH JESUS CHRIST?

That is not my language, yet it is the purpose I have in view. I have just finished a book on prayer, an imaginary correspondence with someone who raises questions about difficulties in prayer.

HOW CAN WE FOSTER THE ENCOUNTER OF PEOPLE WITH JESUS CHRIST?

You can't lay down any pattern for God. There are many different ways of bringing people into his kingdom, even some ways that I specially dislike! I have therefore to be cautious in my judgment.

But we can block it in many ways. As Christians we are tempted to make unnecessary concessions to those outside the faith. We give in too much. Now I don't mean that we should run the risk of making a nuisance of ourselves by witnessing at improper times, but there comes a time when we must show that we disagree. We must show our Christian colors, if we are to be true to Jesus Christ. We cannot remain silent or concede everything away.

There is a character in one of my children's stories named Aslan, who says, "I never tell anyone any story except his own."

I cannot speak for the way God deals with others; I only know how he deals with me personally. Of course, we are to pray for spiritual awakening, and in various ways we can do something toward it.

But we must remember that neither Paul nor Apollos gives the increase. As Charles Williams once said, "The altar must often be built in one place so that the fire may come down in another place."

Do you believe that the Holy Spirit can speak to the world through Christian writers today?

I prefer to make no judgment concerning a writer's direct "illumination" by the Holy Spirit. I have no way of knowing whether what is written is from heaven or not. I do believe that God is the Father of lights— natural lights as well as spiritual lights (see James 1:17). That is, God is not interested only in Christian writers as such. He is concerned with all kinds of writing. In the same way, a sacred calling is not limited to ecclesiastical functions. The man who is weeding a field of turnips is also serving God.

Do you believe that the use of filth and obscenity is necessary in order to establish a realistic atmosphere in contemporary literature?

I do not. I treat this development as a symptom, a sign of a culture that has lost its faith. Moral collapse follows upon spiritual collapse. I look upon the immediate future with great apprehension.

Do you feel, then, that modern culture is being de-Christianized?

I cannot speak to the political aspects of the question, but I have some definite views about the de-Christianizing of the church. I believe that there are many accommodating preachers, and too many practitioners in the church who are not believers. Jesus Christ did not say, "Go into all the world and tell the world that it is quite right."

The gospel is something completely different. In fact, it is directly opposed to the world. The case against Christianity that is made out in the world is quite strong. Every war, every shipwreck, every cancer case, every calamity contributes to making a prima facie case against Christianity. It is not easy to be a believer in the face of this surface evidence. It calls for a strong faith in Jesus Christ.

Do you approve of men such as Billy Graham asking people to come to a point of decision regarding the Christian life?

I had the pleasure of meeting Billy Graham once. We had dinner together during his visit to Cambridge University in 1955, while he was conducting a mission to students. I thought he was a very modest and a very sensible man, and I liked him very much indeed.

In a civilization like ours, I feel that everyone has to come to terms with the claims of Jesus Christ upon his life, or else be guilty of inattention or evading the question. If we refuse to do so, we are guilty of being bad philosophers and bad thinkers.

I have no way of knowing. We have, of
course, the assurance of the New Testament
regarding events to come. I find it difficult
to keep from laughing when I find people
worrying about future destruction of some
kind or other. Didn't they know they were
going to die anyway? Apparently not. My
wife once asked a young woman friend
whether she had ever thought of death, and
she replied, "By the time I reach that age
science will have done something about it."

My primary field is the past. I travel with
my back to the engine, and that makes it difficult to steer. The world might stop in ten
minutes; meanwhile we are to go on doing
our duty. The great thing is to be found
at one's post as a child of God, living each
day as though it were our last, but planning
as though our world might last a hundred
years.

THE GREAT THING IS TO BE FOUND AT ONE'S POST AS A CHILD OF GOD, LIVING EACH DAY AS THOUGH IT WERE OUR LAST, BUT PLANNING AS THOUGH OUR WORLD MIGHT LAST A HUNDRED YEARS. —C. S. LEWIS

LUCY, PETER, & SUSAN

The God of mystery, wonder, and awe becomes "brighter and less blurry."
—C. S. LEWIS, LETTERS TO MALCOM

From the TV program, C. S. Lewis: Beyond Narnia, produced for Faith & Values Media.

7

FOLLOWING THAT BRIGHT BLUR

JERRY ROOT

Jerry Root pastored three different churches over twenty-three years. For ten years while pastoring, he taught courses in philosophy and on C. S. Lewis at the College of DuPage in Glen Ellyn, Illinois. He has been teaching at Wheaton College full-time since 1996. An earlier version of this article first appeared in issue 7 of *Christian History* magazine, and it is used by permission.

Embracing the supernatural elements of Christianity while committed to its rationalism, Lewis brought an orthodox view of a transcendent, immanent God to the common man.

Once in an interview, Elisabeth Elliot was asked, "How could a person deepen his theology and become a clearer thinker?" She answered, "Study the Bible; and study C. S. Lewis. People are always saying C. S. Lewis was not a theologian—and Lewis himself would say that—but he was. He covered the whole field of theology in popular, understandable language. The fact that he could put it in simple language is proof to me that he understood it better than many theologians."[1]

This prescription is helpful. Lewis may not have considered himself a theologian, but his writing on theological subjects has stretched the minds, broadened the hearts, and challenged the thinking of many. The volume, *English Literature in the Sixteenth Century: Excluding Drama,*[2] was Lewis's contribution to the *Oxford History of English Literature*. To write this book Lewis read every book written in English during that century, as well as every book translated into English, in its original language as well as the translation. This was the century of the Reformation; few have read as exhaustively the literature on both sides of the theological debates during that time. Lewis may not have been a theologian, but he was more familiar with some theological literature than most theologians. Furthermore, he was not without theological conviction. He was comfortable with what he called "mere Christianity," and, as for the particulars, he remained an Anglican from the time of his conversion in 1931 until his death in 1963.

What was the core of C. S. Lewis's theology? A hint is found in the caption that appeared below his picture on the cover of the September 8, 1947, *Time* magazine. It simply read, "His heresy: Christianity." Both in written word and BBC broadcasts, Lewis sought to present historic Christian faith to the common man. Perhaps because his work is imaginative as well as analytical, some have criticized him for softness on issues that modern conservatives consider pivotal, for example, biblical authority. Yet those more liberal would be uncomfortable with his unguarded respect for the exclusive claims of Christ. Nevertheless, the cornerstones of his theology are clearly orthodox: again, he called it "mere Christianity" not to diminish the truth claims but to suggest that the truth of God incarnate was so shockingly simple that people of all cultures and pedigrees might be stunned and joyful at its clarity and grace. His public presentations centered in the axiomatic claims common to most Christians, and he left matters on the periphery alone. Of course, one must recognize that debates are likely to arise as to whether or not particular pet interests are really peripheral. Even so, Lewis thought he had a clear idea of historically centrist Christianity, and he deliberately chose to color within these lines.

THE SUPERNATURAL

C. S. Lewis was a committed supernaturalist. In his essay "On Ethics" he commented: "I am myself a Christian, and even a dogmatic Christian untinged with modernist reservations and committed to supernaturalism in its full rigor."[3] Remove the supernatural, and the first principles of Christian orthodoxy are gone. Because God is high and holy, every doctrine of the Christian faith ought to establish in one a sense of awe and wonder, and the miracles that support those doctrines are simply the retelling in capital letters of "the same message which nature writes in her crabbed cursive hand," wrote Lewis.[4] He was fully committed to Christianity with the supernatural elements intact.

Furthermore, Lewis believed that God was greater than what anyone understands of him. He wrote, "All Reality is Iconoclastic."[5] The iconoclast is a breaker of idols. It is possible that one can gain a fresh insight, or image, of God from reading a book, hearing a sermon, or having a conversation with a friend. The image may, in fact, be very helpful; pieces of a larger puzzle begin to take form.

THIS IS CENTRAL TO LEWIS'S THEOLOGY. GOD IS ALWAYS BIGGER THAN WE MIGHT IMAGINE HIM.

ASLAN & LUCY

Nevertheless, the image, as helpful as it once proved to be, if it is held onto too tightly, begins to compete against one's gaining a larger image, or understanding. God is always kicking out the walls of temples built for him, because he wants to give to each a greater grasp of who he is. Lewis observed that God is not so interested in temples built for worshipping him as he is in temples building.[6] Certainly this is what Lucy in the Narnian Chronicles discovered. She had been to Narnia once through the wardrobe. When she returned for a second time, in *Prince Caspian*, and saw the Christ figure, Aslan, for the first time on that return journey, she exclaimed, "Aslan! You're bigger!"[7] She was told by the lion that it was not so, he had not changed, but, in fact, every year she would grow she would find him bigger. This is central to Lewis's theology. God is always bigger than we might imagine him. Good theology keeps that in mind lest it drift towards idolatry.

There are no last words about God, at least for mere mortals. Some are bound to have trouble with this, especially if they confuse the idea of "no last words" with that of "no sure words." Lewis certainly believed one could have a sure word about God, though not a last word. Any truth that one might embrace about God could be plumbed deeper, be applied wider, and also be seen

in coherent relationship with other truths. He writes, "There are three images in my mind which I must continually forsake and replace by better ones: the false image of God, the false image of my neighbours, and the false image of myself."[8] In essence, it is wise for anyone in pursuit of the truth to make it his, or her, motto, "I want God, not my idea of God; I want my neighbor, not my idea of my neighbor; I want myself, not my idea of myself." Lewis's concept of mere Christianity may be exclusive in light of its centrist claims, but it is open to explore more deeply an understanding of God that is never complete. At this point Lewis's love of literature, and his appreciation of the imaginative, was an asset to him.

STUDY OF LITERATURE

Lewis's lifetime study of medieval and renaissance literature also greatly influenced his theological thought. The characteristic that is predominate of that age, he observed, is a commitment to knowledge that was passed along in written form. Lewis commented that, if the medieval "culture is regarded as a response to environment, then the elements in that environment to which it responded most vigorously were manuscripts."[9] This, Lewis writes, is in contrast with more recent

Two jousters in an illuminated manuscript from the Medieval Period.

approaches to the acquisition of knowledge that sees authority as based on personal observation; this is far more individualistic, subjective, and autonomous.[10] He did not believe that individual observations were impossible to make accurately or that they were necessarily unreliable, but to the medieval mind these observations were kept in check by the grand body of knowledge and traditions that preceded them. In his inaugural speech for the chair of Medieval and Renaissance Literature, which had been created for him at Cambridge University, Lewis offered himself to the university not only as a scholar of the medieval era but also as an example of that era. He commented that, "Where I fail as a critic, I may yet be useful as a specimen."[11] He alluded to himself as a kind of dinosaur. What do these matters have to do with his theology?

Actually, they have a great deal to do with his thinking on most matters. He was a man both inside and outside his own time. Perhaps this is why it is so difficult for modern minds, as well as postmoderns, to pigeonhole him, yet his thinking remains so attractive. His broad reading of the past influenced his theology while he lived and continues to be a source of understanding for those who have read him since his death. His orthodoxy belongs to the ages. He was not shy of thinking on his own, he could be original as well as creative, but because he wanted to be accurate whenever he could be, he utilized the wisdom of the past and, where possible, incorporated it into his own theological thought as it developed. Good thinking must be checked not only by one's contemporaries but also by one's predecessors if it is not to go awry. Stuart Barton Babbage commented that Lewis, while speaking to R.A.F. airmen during World War II, would say that doctrines developed over long periods of time, "aren't God: they're only a kind of map. But the map's based on the experience of hundreds of people who really were in touch with God-experiences compared with which any thrills or pious feelings you and I are likely to get on our own are very elementary and very confused. If you want to get further . . . you've got to use a map."[12] Lewis's medieval studies affected him in such

a way that he became a participant in the flow of historic orthodoxy. What's more, he also became an effective communicator of "mere Christianity" to others.

Literary sources also helped him with the insights that truth is one and that good thinking should unify all generations. Authority was weakened by modern emphasis on individual autonomy. Authority rests in the cumulative wisdom of the ages, a demanding jury for all new ideas. Clearly Lewis knew the importance of history, and his theology was bound to the church's historic statements of faith.

IN COMING TO UNDERSTAND ANYTHING WE ARE REJECTING THE FACTS AS THEY ARE FOR US IN FAVOR OF THE FACTS AS THEY ARE.

—C. S. LEWIS

RATIONALISM

Lewis's theology was further influenced by his commitment to logic and reason. Truth was not made for man; man was made for truth. Lewis wrote, "In coming to understand anything we are rejecting the facts as they are for us in favor of the facts as they are."[13] Lewis believed that an objective reality exists external to whatever anyone might think about it. This he called the "Tao" in his book *The Abolition of Man*.[14] Truth is not reality; truth is what one thinks about reality when one things properly about it. Of course everyone is limited in his or her perspective. This is not a liability; it invites one to appreciate the benefits of community and that form of dialogue that can broaden understanding. There is a subjective aspect to truth found in one's response to reality, but there is also a kind of subjectivism that, being unresponsive to truth, seeks to assert one's own way; thus it clouds understanding, destroys community, and Lewis sought to purge this kind of subjectivism from his theology. In this way, if the pursuit of truth is like climbing a ladder, Lewis sought to master the steps as well as turn a floodlight on the ladder itself, illuminating the way so that others, not wishing to remain in the lonely darkness of subjectivism, might follow.[15]

Illumined Subjectivism

As dark subjectivism was a pitfall, illumined subjectivism—he often called it romanticism—could awaken the desire for truth. Lewis would often refer to this desire as joy. Just as hunger says, "I want food," and thirst says, "I want water," so informed joy pleads within a man saying, "I want God." Theology for C. S. Lewis was more than rational activity; it was the burning of the soul not merely to define and explain God but to know him, to enjoy him, and yet to remain constantly in awe of him. He comments, "This hunger is better than any other fullness; this poverty better than all other wealth."[16] Lewis not only sought to explain Christianity to others; he also sought to practice it himself. At the heart of this practice was his personal devotion to God. Theology is not merely about God, nor is it an end in itself. Good theology, properly understood, is about a relationship with God and should lead to a deeper devotion to him.

A comprehensive presentation of Lewis's theology would take a book, perhaps several volumes. Here it is possible to explore briefly two cornerstones of Lewis's theological thought: the transcendence of God and the immanence of God.

Lewis refers to God as the

Bright blur.

God's Transcendence

The idea of God's transcendence is simply this: God is great. His immensity takes into account the fact that he is omnipresent, infinite, and eternal. Though he made the universe, God himself cannot be fully contained in the universe. Where creation leaves off, God goes on and on and on to infinity. In this sense God is incomprehensible. He can never be fully understood by his creatures, a fact that has already been discussed earlier. Because God is transcendent, man is incapable of defining him. The word *definition* means "of the finite." To define a thing is to speak of it in terms of its limitation and its function. Characteristics peculiar to things make it possible to distinguish one thing from another. To be defined a thing must be small enough to wrap words around it. How does one define God? The infinite cannot possibly be reduced to finite definition.[17] In *Letters to Malcolm: Chiefly on Prayer*, Lewis refers to God as the "bright blur,"[18] admitting, as he writes, that this is not a very good description. "In fact," he adds, "you cannot have a good description of anything so vague. If the description became good it would become false."[19] As Walter Elwell has stated, "All theological formulations are, at best, approximate."

The best theology, then, is theology that makes the best approximations. It is necessary, therefore, to choose language equal to the task, and Lewis urges that the best language for this task is poetic. The language of literature is less limiting, is not concerned merely with quantity (as in scientific language) but with quality. Lewis wrote, "To be incommunicable by scientific language is, so far as I can judge, the normal state of experience."[20]

The temptation of the theologian is to adopt language that will be suitable to the scientific mind. However, this kind of language only makes faith less credible. Such language may be suitable to the scientific mind, but it certainly cannot describe God. Lewis insisted that propositional statements about God are necessary. The idea of God, to be understood, must take form in our minds and thought, but if we are to understand the meaning of the propositions, we must go to the language of the poet. Much of the Scriptures are written in poetic form. Lewis understood the value of poetry, metaphor, simile, and story; and he used these as vehicles to consider God in his transcendance.

GOD'S IMMANENCE

The second cornerstone of Lewis's orthodoxy is his commitment to the immanence of God. The infinite, eternal, omnipresent God can and does make his presence known. God can be talked about because God has made himself known to rational creatures capable of reasonable communication. When Lewis was a theist and no more, he thought

it was impossible actually to know God personally and intimately. He understood the concept of transcendence but had not yet balanced it in his thinking with the idea of God's immanence. He commented that he did not think, at that time, that a person could know God any more than Hamlet could know Shakespeare.[21] Later Lewis came to realize that Hamlet could have known Shakespeare, but it could not depend upon Hamlet breaking out of the play to meet the

> WHAT A DISCOVERY! THE GOD OF MYSTERY, WONDER, AND AWE BECOMES "BRIGHTER AND LESS BLURRY."
> —C. S. LEWIS

author, Shakespeare. Nevertheless, as the author of the play, Shakespeare could write himself into the play easily enough as a character, in order to make his presence known to Hamlet. Through this analogy Lewis enables his readers imaginatively to grasp something like what took place in the incarnation. God has made his presence known. Because God has communicated himself to man, man can know and talk about God. Lewis wrote, "Christianity is not merely what a man does with his solitude. It is not even what God does with his solitude. It tells of God descending into the coarse publicity of history and there enacting what can—and must—be talked about."[22]

What a discovery! The God of mystery, wonder, and awe becomes "brighter and less blurry."[23] Lewis wrote, "We may ignore, but we can nowhere evade, the presence of God. The world is crowded with him. He walks everywhere incognito."[24] One might encounter him in this world as readily as one might encounter the lion Aslan in Narnia. As a matter of fact, in Lewis's fiction the incarnation becomes proximate. One feels as if he has tasted and seen that God is near.

CONCLUSION

C. S. Lewis has left a rich theological legacy in the many books he has written. While there is much in his thought, the two ideas of God's transcendence and immanence are the pillars on which rests his "mere Christianity." Lewis has, in many ways, become an everyman's theologian; every man, that is, who hopes to take bearings on the "bright blur."

ENDNOTES:

1. Elisabeth Elliot, *Discipleship Journal*, Issue 8, 1982, 12.

2. C. S. Lewis, *English Literature in the Sixteenth Century: Excluding Drama* (Oxford: Oxford University Press, 1954).

3. C. S. Lewis, *Christian Reflections*, Walter Hooper, ed. (Grand Rapids, Mich.: William B. Eerdmans, 1967), 44.

4. C. S. Lewis, *God in the Dock: Essays in Theology and Ethics*, Walter Hooper, ed. (Grand Rapids, Mich.: William B. Eerdmans, 1970), 29.

5. C. S. Lewis, *A Grief Observed* (London: Faber and Faber, 1966), 56, 60. See also, C. S. Lewis, *Letters to Malcolm: Chiefly on Prayer* (London: Geoffrey Bles, 1964), 109.

6. C. S. Lewis, *Surprised by Joy: The Shape of My Early Life* (New York: Harcourt, Brace and Company, 1955), 167.

7. C. S. Lewis, *Prince Caspian: The Return to Narnia* (London: Fontana, 1980), 124.

8. Walter Hooper, *C. S. Lewis: A Companion Guide* (San Francisco: Harper, 1996), 60. See also, *A Grief Observed*, 56.

9. C. S. Lewis, *The Discarded Image* (Cambridge: Cambridge University Press, 1964), 5.

10. Ibid.

11. C. S. Lewis, *Selected Literary Essays* (Cambridge: Cambridge University Press, 1969), 14.

12. Carolyn Keefe, ed. *C. S. Lewis: Speaker and Teacher* (Grand Rapids, Mich.: Zondervan, 1971), 70–71. See also, C. S. Lewis, *Mere Christianity* (London: Geoffrey Bles, 1964), 122.

13. C. S. Lewis, *An Experiment in Criticism* (Cambridge: Cambridge University Press, 1961), 138.

14. C. S. Lewis, *The Abolition of Man* (San Francisco: Harper, 2001), 18.

15. Lewis writes about the "Poison of Subjectivism" in *Christian Reflections*, 72–81.

16. C. S. Lewis, *The Pilgrim's Regress: An Allegorical Apology for Christianity Reason and Romanticism* (Grand Rapids, Mich.: William B. Eerdmans Publishing Company, 1992), 202.

17. In Lewis's fiction work, *The Great Divorce*, he has George MacDonald observe, "Ye cannot know eternal reality by a definition." C. S. Lewis, *The Great Divorce* (New York: Macmillan, 1946), 129.

18. C. S. Lewis, *Letters to Malcolm*, 110.

19. Ibid.

20. Lewis, *Christian Reflections*, 138.

21. Lewis, *Surprised By Joy*, 227.

22. Lewis, *God in the Dock*, 128.

23. Lewis, *Letters to Malcolm*, 91.

24. Ibid., 75.

PART II

NEW HEAVEN AND EARTH— THE WORLD OF NARNIA

*T*he great creators of metaphor
are the masters of meaning.

—C. S. Lewis, A Preface to
"Paradise Lost"

The original wardrobe from the home of C. S. Lewis, that served as inspiration in
The Lion, the Witch and the Wardrobe.

⚜ 8 ⚜

THROUGH THE WARDROBE: A FAMOUS IMAGE EXPLORED

MICHAEL WARD

The Reverend Michael Ward is chaplain of Peterhouse in the University of Cambridge, England. A former president of the Oxford University C. S. Lewis Society and resident warden of Lewis's Oxford home, The Kilns, Mr. Ward has written and lectured extensively on Lewis's life and works and is currently completing a Ph.D. on Lewis's theological imagination. His publications include "Escape to Wallaby Wood: Lewis's Depictions of Conversion" in *Lightbearer in the Shadowlands: The Evangelistic Vision of C. S. Lewis*, ed. Angus J. L. Menuge and "Planet Narnia," *The Times Literary Supplement*, 25 April 2003. "Through the Wardrobe: A Famous Image Explored" was first published in *Seven: An Anglo-American Literary Review*, vol. 15 (1998).

In Richard Attenborough's film *Shadowlands*, C. S. Lewis and his brother Warren sit in Oxford's Randolph Hotel, awaiting the arrival of Lewis's American correspondent, Joy Gresham. Warren predicts sarcastically, "She'll be writing a dissertation on wardrobes." At the risk of inviting a similar sarcasm, I'm going to write on that very subject because I think the wardrobe was a metaphor of great significance in Lewis's imagination.

Lewis himself observed that "the great creators of metaphor [are] the masters of meaning,"[1] and it's my belief that this wardrobe, the most famous image of the Narnia Chronicles, enables Lewis to master many meanings. Aristotle in his *Poetics* wrote that the ability to make metaphors is a "mark of genius; for to make a good metaphor is to contemplate likeness" (II, xvii, 10). I hope to show that the wardrobe through which the Pevensie children travel has a likeness to several profound things, things that Lewis couldn't have communicated if, instead, he'd written *The Lion, the Witch and the Cupboard* (or *Larder*, or *Water Closet*).

The first thing to point out is that the Narnian wardrobe is not the only important wardrobe in Lewis's writings. There is an earlier one in chapter 17 of *That Hideous Strength*, located in the house of the hero, Ransom: it's not a piece of furniture, but rather a "big room which occupied nearly the whole top floor of one wing at the Manor, and which the Director [Ransom] called the Wardrobe." The novel contains a most interesting scene set in this big upstairs room, and I shall be returning to it below. It should alert us to the possibility that the Narnian wardrobe might serve a deeper purpose than simply that of being a doorway to Lewis's magical land.

THE WARDROBE AS A DOORWAY

But leaving aside Lewis's deeper purposes for the moment, it's in its capacity as a doorway that I wish first to look at the Narnian wardrobe. It's likely that the idea of a wardrobe as an entryway first came to Lewis from one of his favorite children's writers, E. Nesbit. In Nesbit's short story "The Aunt and Anabel," published in *Blackie's Christmas Annual* when Lewis was ten, Anabel finds her way into the magic world through "the station Bigwardrobeinspareroom."

In both Nesbit and Lewis, the wardrobe acts as a doorway. An especially important detail in Lewis's story is his repeated insistence that this doorway must remain open. Five times in the first five chapters of *The Lion, the Witch and the Wardrobe* he alerts his readers to the danger or foolishness of shutting oneself up in a wardrobe. On three of those occasions, Lucy sensibly leaves the door ajar behind her, thinking, "I can always get back if anything goes wrong." On one occasion, it is Peter: "For, of course, he remembered, as every sensible person does, that you should never shut yourself up in a wardrobe." And on the other occasion, it's Edmund, except he does not heed the authorial warning. Eager to ridicule Lucy, he "jumped in and shut the door, forgetting what a very foolish thing this is to do."

I COME INTO THE PRESENCE OF *GOD* WITH A GREAT FEAR LEST ANYTHING SHOULD HAPPEN TO ME WITHIN THAT PRESENCE WHICH WOULD PROVE TOO INTOLERABLY INCONVENIENT WHEN I HAVE COME OUT AGAIN INTO MY "ORDINARY" LIFE . . . —C. S. LEWIS

I assume that Lewis's primary intention here is to warn his child readers so that they don't suffocate or scare themselves when they go looking for Narnia in their own wardrobes, as, I suspect, every child below a certain age does. Indeed, one child in Oxford was found shut up in his parents' wardrobe trying to hack his way into Narnia with a hatchet. But I think there is another, subtler point here too. After all, Lewis's warnings are somewhat laborious: five times in five chapters. He's not usually so heavy-handed.

I believe the warnings are also an ironic tease. Notice how Lewis writes that "sensible" people do not shut themselves up in wardrobes. Being sensible in that kind of scrupulous, overprudential manner is a serious shortcoming in the Narnian scale of virtue. Susan is later criticized for sensibly wanting to be "grown-up" in that way. The point about the open door, which Lewis is making, is explained if we take a look at one of his sermons, where he writes:

I say my prayers, I read a book of devotion, I prepare for, or receive, the Sacrament. But while I do these things there is, so to speak, a voice inside me that urges caution. It tells me to be careful; to keep my head; not to go too far; not to burn my boats. I come into the presence of God with a great fear lest anything should happen to me within that presence which will prove too intolerably inconvenient when I have come out again into my "ordinary" life. . . . This is my endlessly recurrent temptation: to go down to that Sea (I think St. John of the Cross called God a sea) and there neither dive nor swim nor float, but only dabble and splash, careful not to get out of my depth and holding on to the lifeline which connects me with my things temporal.[2]

In *Perelandra* we find a similar passage: "I suppose everyone knows this fear of getting 'drawn in'—the moment at which a man realizes that what had seemed mere speculations are on the point of landing him in the Communist Party or the Christian church —the sense that a door has just slammed and left him on the inside."[3]

Since their visits to Narnia function (among other things) as a preparatory spiritual education for the Pevensie children, it seems clear that it's this natural human ambivalence that Lewis is gently satirizing in his wry warnings not to close the wardrobe door: "Be careful, don't go too far. You want to be sure you can get back if anything goes wrong." The fact that it's the treacherous Edmund who does shut the door behind him only confirms this idea, for Lewis is

EDMUND

DISTANTLY CONNOTES SAUL,

THE AVID

PERSECUTOR

OF THE FIRST

CHRISTIANS.

surely there implying that an enthusiastic hatred of "the spiritual life" or "joy" or "God" or "the church"—however we interpret Lewis's secondary meaning—is better than a lukewarm, Laodicean acceptance, such as Susan's turns out to be. Edmund distantly connotes Saul, the avid persecutor of the first Christians, who became the great apostle, Paul. As Lewis says elsewhere, God is unscrupulous, and a keen atheist cannot be too careful.

THE WARDROBE AS A STOCK OF CLOTHES

The Narnian wardrobe isn't just a doorway; it's also a stock of clothes, so we now turn to consider what meanings Lewis is able to master by way of metaphors drawn from clothing. The place to begin is with the wardrobe's prototype in *That Hideous Strength*. A lengthy quotation will be necessary to give a proper flavor.

That same afternoon Mother Dimble and the three girls were upstairs in the big room which occupied nearly the whole top floor of one wing at the Manor, and which the Director called the Wardrobe. If you had glanced in, you would have thought for one moment that they were not in a room at all but in some kind of

forest—a tropical forest glowing with bright colors. A second glance and you might have thought they were in one of those delightful upper rooms at a big shop where carpets standing on end and rich stuffs hanging from the roof make a kind of woven forest of their own. In fact, they were standing amidst a collection of robes of state—dozens of robes, which hung, each separate, from its little pillar of wood.

"That would do beautifully for you, Ivy," said Mother Dimble lifting with one hand the fold of a vividly green mantle over which thin twists and spirals of gold played in a festive pattern. "Come, Ivy," she continued, "don't you like it?" . . .

"What is it made of?" said Camilla, fingering and then smelling the green mantle. It was a question worth asking. It was not in the least transparent yet all sorts of lights and shades dwelled in its rippling folds and it flowed through Camilla's hands like a waterfall. Ivy became interested.

"Gor!" she said. "However much a yard would it be?"

"There," said Mother Dimble as she draped it skillfully round Ivy. Then she said, "Oh!" in genuine amazement. All three stood back from Ivy staring at her with delight. . . .

"Isn't that like a man!" exclaimed Mrs. Dimble. "There's not a mirror in the room."

"I don't believe we were meant to see ourselves," said Jane. "He said something about being mirrors enough to see one another."

"I would just like to see what I'm like at the back," said Ivy. . . .

"Now Jane," [said Mother Dimble.]

Jane could see nothing specially appropriate in the robe which the others agreed in putting on her. Blue was, indeed, her color but she had thought of something a little more austere and dignified. Left to her own judgment, she would have called this a little "fussy." But when she saw the others all clap their hands, she submitted. Indeed, it did not now occur to her to do otherwise and the whole matter was forgotten a moment later in the excitement of choosing a robe for Mother Dimble.[4]

This quotation comprises less than half of the scene set in the "big upstairs room" or "Wardrobe," and it is the culmination of a major theme in *That Hideous Strength*, a theme that could be designated as "accepting one's given value." The theme appears first in chapter 1 when Jane goes off to buy a hat. We learn there that Jane "liked her clothes to be rather severe and in colors that were really good on serious aesthetic grounds—clothes which would make it plain to everyone that she was an intelligent adult and not a woman of the chocolate-box variety." By buying herself a "seriously aesthetic" hat, Jane is hoping to demonstrate her independent-mindedness. But as she comes out of the hat shop, Jane bumps into Mrs. Dimble. The two women inspect the new hat and "though Mrs. Dimble had really the wrong point of view about such things, there was no denying that the one small alteration which she suggested did go to the root of the matter." So right at the outset, Jane is shown accepting, albeit reluctantly, another person's verdict. Her hat of independence is turning into a helmet of salvation, even here in the first chapter. We have to wait till chapter 14 for her spiritual redemption—in other words, her acceptance of her God-given value. Then in chapter 17, Lewis reprises the whole theme: left to her own judgment, Jane would have called the blue robe, which the others agreed in putting on her, a little fussy. But when she sees the others all clap their hands, she submits.

Submission to the reality of external judgment is foundational to Lewis's spiritual understanding: God is not a projection of our values; he actually exists in his own right, is objectively real. He judges us: we cannot judge him. In an essay entitled "What Are We to Make of Jesus Christ?" Lewis reflects on the frantically comic picture of the fly sitting deciding what it is going to make of the elephant. And in his sermon "The Weight of Glory," he wrote, "I read in a periodical the other day that the fundamental thing is how we think of God. By God himself, it is not! How God thinks of us is not only more important but infinitely more important. Indeed, how we think of him is of no importance except in so far as it is related to how he thinks of us."

SUBMISSION TO THE REALITY OF EXTERNAL JUDGMENT IS FOUNDATIONAL TO LEWIS'S SPIRITUAL UNDERSTANDING: GOD IS NOT A PROJECTION OF OUR VALUES; HE ACTUALLY EXISTS IN HIS OWN RIGHT, IS OBJECTIVELY REAL. HE JUDGES US: WE CANNOT JUDGE HIM.

This principle is cleverly brought out in the wardrobe scene in *That Hideous Strength*. Lewis is drawing on the common human experience of being told that certain clothes suit us or fit us or *are* us. It's an experience many people deliberately invite, never shopping for clothes unless accompanied by someone else as a guide to their choice. In most aspects of life, people dislike being overruled by others, but with clothes, somehow, we tend to hold our own opinions only provisionally. Lewis's technique here, then, is a beautifully simple extrapolation. He points out how, in one department of life—our costume—we acknowledge the existence of a better judge than ourselves. Our guard momentarily down, he punches home the idea of a better judge full-stop. The sartorial, the spiritual: Lewis has contemplated a likeness.

Having considered the main use to which Lewis put the "stock of clothes" imagery in *That Hideous Strength*, I shall now turn to his more developed treatment of it in *The Lion, the Witch and the Wardrobe*. When the four Pevensie children enter the wardrobe, they feel cold and decide to put on the fur coats that they find there:

The coats were rather too big for them so that they came down to their heels and looked more like royal robes than coats when they had put them on. But they all felt a good deal warmer and each thought the others looked better in their new get-up and more suitable to the landscape.[5]

These two sentences are densely packed with metaphoric significance. There are at least three major themes hidden here that could be listed under the headings, personality, pretence, and propriety.

First, PERSONALITY. The robes are like "royal robes," and, of course, in Narnia,

that is just what the four children turn out to be: royal. In putting on the coats, the children realize their true identity; and, that identity is not just a new personal identity but a brave new world in which to live it out—Narnia, a land that is new to them and that starts to be renewed in itself shortly after their arrival. The coincidence of the children's transformation and the transformation of Narnia is not just a literary accident. Lewis really believed, as he wrote in "The Weight of Glory," that men and women are potential "gods and goddesses." Once that potential is realized in Christ, it will be possible for them to "put on" the glory of Nature, "or rather that greater glory of which Nature is only the first sketch."

Lewis's source for these beliefs is, principally, St. Paul, who talks in his second epistle to the Corinthians about the yearning people have for a new individual identity: "Here indeed we groan, and long to put on our heavenly dwelling, so that by putting it on we may not be found naked. For while we are still in this tent, we sigh with anxiety; not that we would be unclothed, but that we would be further clothed, so that what is mortal may be swallowed up by life" (2 Cor. 5:2–4 RSV).

And Paul talks about the yearning of the material world for a new identity in his letter to the Romans: "The creation itself will be set free from its bondage to decay and obtain the glorious liberty of the children of God. We know that the whole creation has been groaning in travail together until now" (Rom. 8:21–22 RSV).

Both humanity and the created world are groaning, and their release from that groaning, according to Paul, is a joint release, which is what Lewis dramatizes with his clothing imagery because not only do the Pevensie children put on fur coats but Narnia itself puts off its wintry whiteness: we read a few pages later, "Every moment more and more of the trees shook off their robes of snow." By combining these changes in identity, Lewis imaginatively presents a rounded version of resurrection doctrine, a doctrine he addressed more directly in *Miracles*:

CHRISTIANITY DOES NOT TEACH US TO DESIRE A TOTAL RELEASE [FROM THE MATERIAL WORLD]. WE DESIRE, LIKE ST. PAUL, NOT TO BE UNCLOTHED BUT TO BE RECLOTHED: TO FIND NOT THE FORMLESS EVERYWHERE-AND-NOWHERE BUT THE PROMISEDLAND, THAT NATURE WHICH WILL BE ALWAYS AND PERFECTLY—AS PRESENT NATURE IS PARTIALLY AND INTERMITTENTLY—THE INSTRUMENT FOR THAT MUSIC WHICH WILL THEN ARISE BETWEEN CHRIST AND US.[6]

The fur coats go on the children; the robes of snow come off the trees. In this way the clothing imagery gives us much more than a narrowly individualistic understanding of personality: the whole of creation is involved. As Lewis put it in his address entitled "Membership," paraphrasing Galatians 6:15: "Christianity is not, in the long run, concerned either with individuals or communities. Neither the individual nor the community as popular thought understands them can inherit eternal life: neither the natural self, nor the collective mass, but a new creature." So it is that Lewis goes "beyond personality," suggesting a wholesale Narnian redemption. The individual is renewed as each child puts on the coat prepared for him or her; the community is renewed because these coats are royal coats, showing that Narnian society is a rightful monarchy once more, not a dictatorship; and the environment itself is renewed as the landscape sloughs off its wintry skin.

The second meaning we find in the Narnian wardrobe is PRETENSE. Notice the phrase Lewis uses about the coats being "rather too big for them." In terms of the story, this is as we would expect: after all, the Pevensies have not yet been enthroned. They may be royal: they are not yet kings and queens. But in a broader context, this idea is much more meaningful. As Lewis writes in *Mere Christianity*:

[The first words of the Lord's Prayer] are Our Father. Do you now see what those words mean? They mean quite frankly, that you are putting yourself in the place of a son of God. To put it bluntly, you are dressing up as Christ. If you like, you are pretending. Because, of course, the moment you realize what the words mean, you realize that you are not a son of God. . . . So that, in a way, this dressing up as Christ is a piece of outrageous cheek. But the odd thing is that He has ordered us to do it.

Why? What is the good of pretending to be what you are not? Well, even on the human level, you know, there are two kinds of pretending. There is a bad kind, where the pretence is there instead of the real thing; as when a man pretends he is going to help you instead of really helping you. But there is also a good kind, where the pretence leads up to the real thing. When you are not feeling particularly friendly but know you ought to be, the best thing you can do, very often, is to put on a friendly manner and behave as if you were a nicer person than you actually are. And in a few minutes, as we have all noticed, you will be really feeling friendlier than you were. Very often the only way to get a quality in reality is to start behaving as if you had it already. That is why children's games are so important. They are always pretending to be grown-ups—playing soldiers, playing shop. But all the time, they are hardening their muscles and sharpening their wits, so that the pretence of being grown-up helps them to grow up in earnest.[7]

Again Lewis's source is Paul, who writes in various epistles such things as "put on the armor of light," "put on Christ," "put on the new man," "put on charity." The

LUCY, PETER, SUSAN, & EDMUND

VERY OFTEN THE ONLY WAY TO GET A QUALITY IN REALITY IS TO START BEHAVING AS IF YOU HAD IT *A*LREADY.

Pevensies are called upon to behave as kings and queens long before their coronation: their willingness and ability to act royally enable them to become royal indeed. In other words, they are required to become what they are.

Note how, at the end of the book, when they apologize to Professor Kirke for losing four of his fur coats, he tells them, "I don't think it will be any good trying to go back through the wardrobe door to get the coats.

You won't get into Narnia again by that route. Nor would the coats be much use by now if you did!" This means, I think, that the coats have served their purpose of helping the children to grow up spiritually and that there is now no more reason to put them on again than there would be to wear a fur coat once winter is over. The children have hardened their muscles and sharpened their wits; it is time to move on to a new lesson.

And the third meaning that Lewis opens up by means of the Narnian wardrobe is PROPRIETY: "each thought the others looked better in their new get-up and more suitable to the landscape." Well, yes, of course, a fur coat is suitable to winter landscape, but I suspect that Lewis also has in mind that royal raiment is suitable to a monarch in his own realm. It is a question of appropriateness. A sovereign, being regal, ought to look regal. Lewis makes this point in his *A Preface to Paradise Lost* in the chapter defending Milton's style. Milton had chosen a grand theme, the fall of man, and therefore, Lewis argues, a grand style is appropriate.

A man performing a rite is not trying to make you think that this is his natural way of walking, these the unpremeditated gestures of his own domestic life. If long usage has in fact made the ritual unconscious, he must labor to make it look deliberate, in order that we, the assistants, may feel the weight of solemnity pressing on his shoulders as well as on our own. Anything casual or familiar in his manner is not "sincerity" or "spontaneity," but impertinence. Even if his robes were not heavy in fact, they ought to look heavy.[8]

It was Lewis's belief that style was part of content and that, at bottom, every ideal of style dictates not only how we should say things but what sort of things we may say. In terms of personal wardrobes then, this presumably means that if there should be no such thing as regal apparel, there may be no such thing as a sovereign. For this reason Lewis labors to give a regal aura to the clothes worn by his Narnian kings and queens. The more fitting their costumes appear to be, the more their royalty will stand forth. In *The Silver Chair*, Eustace and Jill are given "suitable clothes . . . in the most honorable fashion"; and in *Prince Caspian* we find this description: "The children and the Dwarfs had made good use of the royal wardrobes . . . and what with the silk and cloth of gold, with snowy linen glancing through slashed sleeves, with silver mail shirts and jeweled sword-hilts, with gilt helmets and feathered bonnets, they were almost too bright to look at." In an age in which everyone puts on his oldest clothes to be happy in, Lewis is attempting to reawaken us to "the simpler state of mind in which people put on gold and scarlet to be happy in."

Your taste for fine clothes is an indication of your spiritual standing, in Lewis's view. Since Christian men and women are sons and daughters of the King of kings, they are, as a result, princes and princesses whose liking for gold and scarlet clothes should be natural and inevitable. Throughout his Narnian books, and indeed, everywhere in his writing, Lewis uses clothes as an index of spiritual health.

For instance, in *The Lion, the Witch and the Wardrobe*, Edmund, when he deserts the Beavers' house, leaves his royal robe behind him, a clear picture of his conversion to the witch's side. In *The Voyage of the Dawn Treader*, there is an important emphasis on clothes in the episode of Eustace's undragoning. Aslan tells Eustace that he must undress in order to ease the pain in his leg. Three times Eustace tries to remove his dragon skin, without success. Then the lion says, "You will have to let me undress you," and he tears the dragon-skin off Eustace like it's a huge scab. Eustace, having told all this to Edmund, then reveals that:

"The lion took me out and dressed me—"

THREE TIMES EUSTACE TRIES TO REMOVE HIS DRAGON SKIN, WITHOUT SUCCESS.
THEN THE LION SAYS, "YOU WILL HAVE TO LET ME *U*NDRESS YOU,"
AND HE TEARS THE DRAGON-SKIN OFF EUSTACE LIKE IT'S A HUGE SCAB.

"Dressed you. With his paws?" says Edmund.

"Well, I don't exactly remember that bit. But he did somehow or other: in new clothes—the same I've got on now, as a matter of fact. And then suddenly I was back here. Which is what makes me think it must have been a dream."

"No. It wasn't a dream," said Edmund.

"Why not?"

"Well, there are the clothes, for one thing. And you have been—well, undragoned, for another."[9]

EUSTACE

Again, Lewis is echoing to Paul: "We desire not to be un-clothed, but to be further clothed." If there remains any doubt about the importance of this metaphor to Lewis, it should be laid to rest by looking at the epitaph he wrote for his wife:

Here the whole world (stars, water, air,
And field, and forest, as they were
Reflected in a single mind)
Like cast off clothes was left behind
In ashes yet with hope that she,
Re-born from holy poverty,
In lenten lands, hereafter, may
Resume them on her Easter Day.[10]

To summarize; the wardrobe in the sense of "a stock of clothes" not only provides Lewis with a useful metaphorical way of talking about external judgment, it also symbolizes personality, pretense, and propriety, conversion, and even resurrection.

The Wardrobe as a Doorway in a Stock of Clothes

Lewis indirectly explains the usefulness of clothing as a spiritual metaphor in *The Four Loves* where he writes, in the chapter on erotic love:

The word naked was originally a past participle; the naked man was the man who had undergone the process of naking, that is, of stripping or peeling. . . . Time out of mind the naked man has seemed to our ancestors not the natural but the abnormal man; not the man who has abstained from dressing but the man who has been for some reason undressed. And it is a simple fact . . . that nudity emphasizes common humanity and soft-pedals what is individual. In that way we are "more ourselves" when clothed. By nudity the lovers cease to be solely John and Mary; the universal He and She are emphasized. You could almost say they put on nakedness as a ceremonial robe.[11]

Clothes are a useful spiritual symbol because we are "more ourselves" when clothed. However, it is undeniably the case that clothes mask as well as adorn. What about "the universal He and She"? That, being a good thing, must also be symbolized if Lewis wishes to present an orthodox picture of the redeemed or resurrected life. The collective mass and the individual person are involved in the new creature. Although clothes provide Lewis with such a wealth of imagery, they are, after all, only medicine for fallen man, only a post-garden of Eden necessity. As he wrote in a magazine article entitled "Equality": "Clothes are good because we are no longer innocent. . . . We must wear clothes since the Fall. Yes, but inside, under what Milton called 'these troublesome disguises,' we want the naked body, that is, the real body, to be alive." And Lewis makes the point again in his essay "Membership": "It is the naked body, still there beneath the clothes of each one of us, which really lives."

Is Lewis contradicting himself? On the one hand, he says that "we are more ourselves when clothed"; on the other he says that it is only the naked body which really lives. Which is it? I think the answer is both. Mankind has contradicted itself by falling. In the ideal, unfallen state, nudity expressed all that needed to be said about the human person, and Lewis is content to depict the Green Lady in *Perelandra* as naked because she is still in a state of innocence. But mankind is fallen, and simply to revert to paradisal nakedness is not an option. If human actions are to have any significance, they cannot simply be undone. The whole methodology of Christianity is not simply to reverse evil but to transcend it, going through evil and coming out the other side: resurrection, not resuscitation. And this resurrection life is what Lewis attempts to depict by counterbalancing ideas of clothing

and nudity and so achieving a paradoxical state that gets somewhere near the truth. And it's this paradox that I shall be looking at in the remainder of this essay.

We see a hint of the paradox toward the end of *The Last Battle* in the juxtaposition of Tirian and Puzzle. Tirian "felt awkward about coming among [the great Kings and Queens of Narnia] with the blood and dust and sweat of a battle still on him. Next moment he realized that he was not in that state at all. He was fresh and cool and clean, and dressed in such clothes as he would have worn for a great feast at Cair Paravel. (But in Narnia your good clothes were never your uncomfortable ones. They knew how to make things that felt beautiful as well as looking beautiful in Narnia: and there was no such thing as starch or flannel or elastic to be found from one end of the country to the other)." So Tirian is reclothed. Puzzle the donkey, in contrast, is unclothed: "'Why, it's old Puzzle!' They had never seen him by daylight with the lion-skin off, and it made an extraordinary difference. He was himself now: a beautiful donkey with such a soft, grey coat, and such a gentle, honest face." Here Lewis nods in the direction of the nude half of the paradox (if you can describe an animal as being nude), but no more.

Perhaps the clearest presentation of the paradox comes in *The Great Divorce*, in the

heavenly vision of a great lady (her name is Sarah Smith) in whose honor a procession is being held:

I cannot now remember whether she was naked or clothed. If she were naked, then it must have been the almost visible penumbra of her courtesy and joy which produces in my memory the illusion of a great and shining train that followed her across the happy grass. If she were clothed, then the illusion of nakedness is doubtless due to her charity with which her inmost spirit shone through the clothes. For clothes in that country are not a disguise: the spiritual body lives along each thread and turns them into living organs. A robe or a crown is there as much one of the wearer's features as a lip or an eye.[12]

I wonder whether Lewis did not create Sarah Smith as a result of thinking about Christ's transfiguration. We know something of what he thought about it from a passage in *Miracles* where he speculates that the metamorphosis of Jesus was an anticipatory glimpse of heavenly reality:

The change which His own human form had undergone is described as one to luminosity, to "shining whiteness." A similar whiteness characterizes His appearance at the beginning of the book of Revelation. One rather curious detail is that this shining or whiteness affected His clothes as much as His body. St. Mark indeed mentions the clothes more explicitly than the face, and adds, with inimitable naivety, that "no laundry could do anything like it." . . . We do not know to what phase or feature of the New Creation this episode points. It may . . . reveal a glory which all risen men will inherit. We do not know.[13]

At any rate, Lewis is obviously intrigued by the fact that Christ's Transfiguration transfigured both clothes and body, and in the depiction of Sarah Smith in *The Great Divorce* he comes closer than anywhere else to recreating it explicitly in his fiction.

Explicitly, I say, because of course the crowning success of the Narnian wardrobe as a symbol is that it allows Lewis to recreate this transfiguration implicitly. The Narnian wardrobe is not just a doorway, nor just a stock of clothes; *it is a doorway in a stock of clothes*, a fact so obvious that it might be thought the first and least important thing to say, when in fact it is the last and most important thing, the culminating purpose for which Lewis invented it, as is suggested by the fact that this is the principal way in which the wardrobe differs from the earlier one in *That Hideous Strength*. By being a doorway in a stock of clothes, the Narnian wardrobe allows the imagination almost literally to go beyond concepts of clothing and nudity. As Lewis wrote in "The Weight of Glory":

WE ARE SUMMONED TO PASS IN THROUGH NATURE, BEYOND HER, INTO THAT SPLENDOR WHICH SHE FITFULLY REFLECTS. . . .

AT PRESENT WE ARE ON THE OUTSIDE OF THE WORLD, THE WRONG SIDE OF THE DOOR. . . .

WE CANNOT MINGLE WITH THE SPLENDORS WE SEE. BUT ALL THE LEAVES OF THE NEW TESTAMENT ARE RUSTLING WITH THE RUMOR THAT IT WILL NOT ALWAYS BE SO. SOME DAY, GOD WILLING, WE SHALL GET IN. . . .

THE DOOR ON WHICH WE HAVE BEEN KNOCKING ALL OUR LIVES WILL OPEN AT LAST.[14]

That passage gains new weight if we read it with Lewis's most famous image in mind: "Then everyone looked in and pulled the coats apart; and they all saw—Lucy herself saw—a perfectly ordinary wardrobe. There was no wood and no snow, only the back of the wardrobe, with hooks on it. Peter went in and rapped his knuckles on it to make sure."[15]

On that occasion the children gained no admittance, but the Christian revelation taught Lewis to believe that he who seeks finds, and to him who knocks it will be opened. Some day, God willing, the back of the wardrobe will swing wide; and both body and clothes will be transfigured. The shame of nakedness and the disguise of dress will vanish. In their place the individual John and Mary will appear inseparable from the universal He and She.

"'This must be a simply enormous wardrobe!' thought Lucy, going still farther in and pushing the soft folds of the coats aside to make room for her." That sentence encapsulates the whole paradox. As Lucy goes further into the home of clothes, she pushes clothes aside. Lewis depicted many such oxymorons in his attempts to give a taste of heaven: for instance, the sweet sea in the *Dawn Treader*, and the onion-ring worlds within worlds in *The Last Battle*. But I suggest that the wardrobe is the most masterly of his metaphors, the fullest with meaning and deservedly the most famous. As a simple doorway the wardrobe takes its place in the tradition of English children's fiction alongside other famous entryways to magical lands, such as Carroll's looking glass and Rowling's platform nine and three quarters. As a stock of clothes it provides images of judgment, personality, pretense, propriety, redemption, and resurrection. Finally, as a doorway in a stock of clothes, it suggests a likeness to that spiritual reality longed for by the great apostle and apparently demonstrated by Christ, which is this (to paraphrase Lewis): that neither the naked nor the dressed as popular thought understands them can inherit eternal life; neither the nude nor the clothed, but a new creature; neither outside the wardrobe, nor inside the wardrobe, but through the wardrobe—with the door closed for good and all behind.

ENDNOTES:

1. C. S. Lewis, "Bluspels and Flalansferes: A Semantic Nightmare," first published in *Rehabilitations and Other Essays* (Oxford: Oxford University Press, 1939); reprinted in *Selected Literary Essays* (Cambridge: Cambridge University Press, 1969), 251–65.

2. C. S. Lewis, "A Slip of the Tongue," sermon preached in Magdalene College, Cambridge, 1956; reprinted in *C. S. Lewis, Essay Collection*, ed. Lesley Walmsley (New York: HarperCollins, 2000), 384–87.

3. C. S. Lewis, *Perelandra* (New York: Scribners, 1996), chapter 1.

4. C. S. Lewis, *That Hideous Strength* (New York: Scribners, 1996), chapter 17, section 2.

5. C. S. Lewis, *The Lion, the Witch and the Wardrobe* (Harmondsworth, Middlesex, England: Penguin Books, 1959), chapter 6.

6. C. S. Lewis, *Miracles: A Preliminary Study* (San Francisco: HarperSanFrancisco, 2001), chapter 16.

7. C. S. Lewis, *Mere Christianity* (New York: Macmillan, 1960), book 4, chapter 7.

8. C. S. Lewis, *A Preface to "Paradise Lost"* (Oxford: Oxford University Press, 1942), chapter 8.

9. C. S. Lewis, *The Voyage of the Dawn Treader* (New York: Harper Trophy, 1994), chapter 7.

10. C. S. Lewis, "Epitaph for Helen Joy Davidman," *Collected Poems* (New York: HarperCollins, 1994), 252.

11. C. S. Lewis, *The Four Loves* (New York: Harvest Books, 1971), chapter 5.

12. C. S. Lewis, *The Great Divorce* (New York: Macmillan, 1946), 97–98.

13. Lewis, *Miracles*, chapter 16.

14. C. S. Lewis, "The Weight of Glory," sermon preached in the University Church of St. Mary the Virgin, Oxford, 1941; reprinted in *C. S. Lewis, Essay Collection*, ed. Lesley Walmsley (New York: HarperCollins, 2000), 96–106.

15. Lewis, *The Lion, the Witch and the Wardrobe*, chapter 3.

A wardrobe that opens to the transcendent incarnate that is Christ Jesus born in a stable is a portal to paradise.

—Angus Menuge

9

FROM THE WARDROBE TO THE STABLE: LEWIS'S DEFENSE OF THE TRANSCENDENT INCARNATE

ANGUS MENUGE

Angus Menuge is professor of philosophy at Concordia University Wisconsin and associate director of the Cranach Institute at Concordia Theological Seminary, Fort Wayne, Indiana. He is the editor of three books (one on C. S. Lewis) and the author of two, his most recent being *Agents Under Fire: Materialism and the Rationality of Science.*

In both his imaginative writings and his apologetics, Lewis argued that the true meaning of life transcends the categories of everyday experience. He was concerned about refuting a pervasive modern secularism, which limits reality to the natural and knowledge to the results of materialistic science. According to this view, we are imprisoned in a universe devoid of intrinsic meaning or purpose, like a child trapped in a typical wardrobe, finding only a wall of solid wood at the back. When Lewis describes a magic wardrobe that enables children to access Narnia, he thereby asserts that we do not inhabit a closed system of natural causes but a porous world, shot through with transcendence.

But Lewis does not argue for some

> WHEN LEWIS DESCRIBES A MAGIC WARDROBE THAT ENABLES CHILDREN TO ACCESS NARNIA, HE THEREBY ASSERTS THAT WE DO NOT INHABIT A CLOSED SYSTEM OF NATURAL CAUSES BUT A POROUS WORLD, SHOT THROUGH WITH TRANSCENDENCE.

vague spirituality. He defends orthodox Christianity, in which a transcendent God becomes incarnate as a human being. To do this he combats the errors of a liberal civil religion, which claims that various revealed religions, such as Christianity and Islam, are merely different ways of presenting the same God and can easily be united (syncretism). Lewis's critique of syncretism culminates in the stable of *The Last Battle*, where Tash is revealed as a demonic power and Aslan, the Christ figure of Narnia, presides over a final judgment, drawing believers into paradise.

The great debate between orthodox Christianity and its secular and religious debunkers continues throughout The Chronicles of Narnia. We will follow this debate from the wardrobe of the second chronicle all the way to the stable of the last. In the process we will notice that Lewis not only evokes the transcendent incarnate; he also defends it.

THE WARDROBE: DEAD END OR PORTAL TO TRANSCENDENCE?

One of the experiences that inspired Lewis to write The Chronicles of Narnia was his observation of young evacuees from London who stayed at his house during World War II. Lewis noticed that the children lived only in the world of immediate experience, were lacking in imagination, unschooled in Christian doctrine, and closed to the transcendent. In fact they were not so different from the Pevensie children described in *The Lion, the Witch and the Wardobe*. By drawing readers to identify with these children, Lewis hopes the reader will overcome the same resistance to the transcendent.

When the Pevensie children first visit the professor's house, all except Lucy have a prejudice against possibilities that transcend their everyday experience. When Lucy claims to have found another country through the back of a wardrobe, they immediately suppose that she is either lying or mentally unbalanced. They assume that these are the only possibilities even though all their actual evidence counts against both of them. (Lucy is honest and perfectly coherent.) They do not seriously consider a third possibility,

that Lucy is telling the truth, even though it better fits the evidence, for given their background philosophy such a thing "couldn't be true."[1] For them, the universe is a closed system, like a "perfectly ordinary wardrobe" with a back on it.[2]

However, the professor protests that their philosophy has closed their minds to the true logic of the situation. Lewis is arguing that modern secularism leads to a bias that will dismiss claims for the transcendent (the existence of God, objective morality, miracles, "intelligent design") even if they are well-supported by facts and logic. When the professor complains, "Why don't they teach logic at these schools?"[3] Lewis voices his own belief that modern education is to blame.

IDEAS HAVE CONSEQUENCES

An inadequate emphasis on critical thinking is not the only problem. Lewis argues that the secularization of education leads to a built-in bias against the transcendent. This is an important theme in *Prince Caspian*. When Miraz usurps the throne, he is eager to start a line of kings independent of Aslan. Rejecting Aslan's authority, he seeks to suppress all the stories that connect him to Narnia's history. Since Aslan is the Christ figure of The Chronicles, Miraz's

program is one of secularized revisionist history. Miraz requires teachers to reject the old stories of Aslan as myths, no matter how well attested. When he discovers that the young Caspian's nurse has told him of the great lion, Miraz responds with Orwellian censorship: "Never let me catch you talking—or *thinking* either—about all those silly stories again. . . . There's no such person as Aslan. And there are no such things as lions."[4] The nurse is summarily dismissed. An educational system that only presents secular accounts of reality inherently favors modern secularism over religious perspectives. Since students are only allowed to think along secular paths, they will easily, though erroneously, identify rationality with secular thought. The abstract logical possibility of the transcendent will not suffice to gain it a fair hearing.

We learn that a centralized educational system can be highly effective at propagating a secular bias. Miss Prizzle, one of Miraz's loyal teachers, taught "'History' that was . . . duller than the truest history you ever read and less true than the most exciting adventure story."[5] When brought face-to-face with Aslan, Miss Prizzle, and all of her class except Gwendolen, preferred flight from the transcendent incarnate to an acknowledgment of its existence.[6] Seeing is not believing, for as Lewis argued, "Whatever experiences we may have, we shall not regard them as miraculous if we already hold a philosophy which excludes the supernatural."[7] The same holds not only for miracles but for any signs of the transcendent. If a worldview that denies the possibility of transcendence has been inculcated, any experience that points beyond the natural world can be explained away. "If the modern materialist saw with his own eyes the heavens rolled up and the great white throne appearing, if he had the sensation of being himself hurled into the Lake of Fire, he would continue forever, in that lake itself, to regard his experience as an illusion and to find the explanation of it in psycho-analysis, or cerebral pathology."[8]

Lewis critiques the same kind of secular education this side of the wardrobe. In *The Voyage of the Dawn Treader* we are introduced to Eustace Clarence Scrubb, who is impressed with modern science and technology but is morally and spiritually atrophied, a "man without a chest."[9] As a result, Eustace is unable to accept the ideas of moral values that transcend humanistic ideas of progress and is closed to the idea of God. This is partly because he had read "only the wrong books. They had a lot to say about exports and imports and governments and drains, but they were weak on dragons."[10] It is also because of Eustace's smugly progressive parents, Harold and Alberta, who were "very up-to-date . . . and wore a special kind of underclothes."[11]

And finally, we learn in *The Silver Chair* that Eustace has been sent to "Experiment House," a modernist school where bullies are "interesting psychological cases"[12] who go unpunished, and "Bibles were not encouraged."[13] The pupils of this school are viewed as experimental subjects who are conditioned in secular thought that serves the interests of the state. Like Miss Prizzle, the head of Experiment House cannot accept the transcendent incarnate in front of her face: "When she saw the lion and the broken wall and Caspian and Jill and Eustace . . . she had hysterics and . . . began ringing up the police with stories about a lion escaped from a circus, and escaped convicts who broke down walls and carried drawn swords."[14] She said this even though the police found no evidence to support her story and even though her own crazed behavior suggested she did not believe it herself but was desperately repressing what she really knew.

All of this is in stark contrast to Christian education. Despite the censorship of Miraz, Doctor Cornelius meets Prince Caspian in secret and tells him, "All you have heard about Old Narnia is true. It is not the country of Men. It is the country of Aslan. . . . of Talking Beasts."[15] Dr. Cornelius thereby rejects the hubris of modern secularism,

ALL YOU HAVE HEARD ABOUT OLD NARNIA IS TRUE. IT IS NOT THE COUNTRY OF MEN. IT IS THE COUNTRY OF ASLAN. . . . OF TALKING BEASTS.

—DR. CORNELIUS

YOU SEE, ASLAN
DIDN'T TELL POLE
WHAT WOULD
HAPPEN. HE ONLY
TOLD HER WHAT
TO DO.
—PUDDLEGLUM

which makes human beings masters of reality and asserts instead that God is the King over all creatures. Likewise in *The Silver Chair*, Aslan catechizes Jill Pole with four signs, four promises of God, which are to be believed in faith even when they seem contrary to ordinary experience. When Jill, Eustace, and Puddleglum are searching for Prince Rilian, they encounter the last sign from the lips of an apparent madman bound to a silver chair. In his plea for freedom, he is the first person in their travels to invoke the name of Aslan, yet setting him loose threatens all of their lives. After various attempts to evade the sign, Puddleglum prevails: "You see, Aslan didn't tell Pole what would happen. He only told her what to do. That fellow will be the death of us once he's up, I shouldn't wonder. But that doesn't let us off following the sign."[16]

It turns out that the captive was none other than Prince Rilian, who had been trapped in the enchanted deceptions of the witch of Underland. The children learn to trust God's transcendent promises by faith and not by sight (2 Cor. 5:7).

Yet the witch of Underland's revisionist education almost succeeds in blotting out transcendence. She employs the classic debunking strategy of the secular reductionist. Given any feature of reality that appears to transcend the secular, such as objective morality or the divine, the reductionist proposes a material surrogate instead. Today evolutionary psychologists claim that our moral intuitions do not reveal a moral law but reflect the interests of our "selfish genes." And recently some have even proposed a "God gene," to explain away religious belief. In the same way, the witch of Underland tries to convince the children and Puddleglum that their departure from her castle is futile because Underland is all there is. If Underland is identified with the material world, then she is saying that all of reality is like the closed system of an ordinary wardrobe with a back on it, and that anything that appears to transcend this system must be an illusion.

When Puddleglum protests that there is a sun in the land above and compares this sun to a lamp in the room, the witch argues that the idea of the sun is only copied from the lamp, which is all there really is.

"You see? When you try to think out clearly what this *sun* must be, you cannot tell me. You can only tell me it is like the lamp. Your *sun* is a dream; and there is nothing in that dream that was not copied from the lamp. The lamp is the real thing; the *sun* is but a tale, a children's story."[17]

Likewise it is claimed that the idea of Aslan is copied from an ordinary cat. The strategy is generalized to all ideas of the transcendent:

"You can put nothing into your make-believe without copying it from the real world, this world of mine, which is the only world."[18]

The enchantment is almost complete when Puddleglum counteracts it by stamping in the witch's fire and replying to her debunking philosophy. "Suppose this black pit of a kingdom of yours *is* the only world. Well, it strikes me as a pretty poor one. And that's a funny thing, when you come to think of it. We're just babies making up a game, if you're right. But four babies playing a game can make a play-world which licks your real world hollow."[19]

The argument is left rather implicit, but Lewis is clearly attacking the intelligibility of the debunker's claim that our ideas of "higher" things can derive from "lower" sources. How can the idea of something great derive from something lacking that greatness? Could the idea of eternity arise from the materialist's temporal world? Could the ideas of infinity and perfection derive from the finite, imperfect world of the materialist? Could the idea of a necessary being like God derive from the materialist's contingent universe? There is a good case to be made that material causes do not account for the content of these ideas. It takes a strong Christian education, evident in Puddleglum's discerning judgment, to see through the enchantment of secular reductionism.

NO DOUBT . . . WHEN THEY SPEAK OF HIM AS A LION THEY ONLY MEAN HE'S AS STRONG AS A LION OR (TO OUR ENEMIES, OF COURSE) AS FIERCE AS A LION. . . . —BREE

THE DECEPTIONS OF LIBERAL THEOLOGY

Modern secularism is not the only enemy of orthodox Christianity. Many are open to the transcendent but cannot face the implications of the incarnation, that God himself became a human being in the same grimy history that we inhabit. Behind this may be a curious sort of arrogance that makes people more "spiritual" than God. We see this in *The Horse and His Boy*, where the proud talking warhorse Bree falls into Docetism. Docetism, a heresy combated by the early church, claims that God can only be transcendent and therefore only seemed to become man. Thus Bree argues that Aslan is not really a lion;[20] and while Aslan himself appears and approaches from behind, Bree explains (in the condescending manner of the Episcopal Ghost of *The Great Divorce*):

"No doubt . . . when they speak of him as a Lion they only mean he's as strong as a lion or (to our enemies, of course) as fierce as a lion. . . . Even a little girl like you, Aravis, must see that it would be quite absurd to suppose he is a *real* lion. Indeed it would be disrespectful. If he was a lion he'd have to be a Beast just like the rest of us. Why! . . . If he was a lion he'd have four paws, and a tail, and Whiskers! . . . Aie, ooh, hoo-hoo! Help!"[21]

In a manner strongly reminiscent of Jesus' response to doubting Thomas, Aslan allows Bree to touch him and smell him and says, "Here are my paws, here is my tail, these are my whiskers. I am a true Beast."[22] Christianity requires more than recognition of transcendence. We must also see that our Savior is the God-Man Christ Jesus, the transcendent incarnate. Our human pride makes us think that through our own spirituality and righteousness we can reach up to God. But the truth is that we are by nature enemies of God (Rom. 8:7–8) and that he must reach down to us in Christ, fulfilling all righteousness in his active obedience, and taking the punishment we deserve for our sins in his passive obedience. The idea that only God himself can bridge the gap between God and man is unique to Christianity.

Nonetheless we suffer today from doctrinal indifference and the well-meaning hope that we would all get along much better in a pluralist society if the various religions were held to be equivalent. Sometimes this appears as the view that each religion is an equally valid path up the same mountain of salvation (indifferentism), while at others it

HERE ARE MY PAWS, HERE IS MY TAIL, THESE ARE MY WHISKERS. I AM A TRUE BEAST.—ASLAN

is claimed we can forge a new, more inclusive "civil religion," by synthesizing elements from the traditional, revealed religions (syncretism). Both claims are in conflict with the Bible and with logic. The Bible clearly teaches that there is only one true God (Deut. 6:4; I Cor. 8:4), that he is a jealous God who tolerates no rivals (Exod. 20:3; Deut. 5:7), and that he is triune (Matt. 28:19), yet Islam denies the Trinity. Likewise the Bible tells us that Jesus is not *a* way but the *only* way of salvation (John 14:6; I Tim. 2:5), while other religions deny that Jesus is required at all. Islam, for example, denies the incarnation, crucifixion, and resurrection of Jesus, saying that he is only an important prophet, and claims that we are saved by our good deeds outweighing our bad deeds (by works and not by grace).

We see this theme play out in *The Last Battle*. Shift the Ape serves as the antichrist of Narnia's end-times, dressing a donkey in a lion skin to impersonate Aslan while claiming to be Aslan's interpreter. In fact, Shift does not believe in Aslan, but he does believe that Aslan's powerful name can be used to manipulate others for personal gain, persuading the Narnians to surrender Narnia's assets to the Calormenes. It is fairly clear from its characterization in *The Horse and His Boy* that Calormen is the Narnian equivalent of an Islamic state, although by the time of *The Last Battle*, it has largely fallen away from Tash. In an atmosphere of doctrinal weakness and indifferentism, Shift is able to maximize his appeal to both Narnians and Calormenes by proposing a syncretic fusion of Tash and Aslan. He argues, "Tash is only another name for Aslan. . . . Tash is Aslan: Aslan is Tash."[23] Tirian is unable to tell by sight if the creature that appears nightly outside the stable is Aslan, but he discerns by faith and sound doctrine that it is a fraud. For there is no way that "the terrible god Tash who fed on the blood of his people could possibly be the same as the good Lion by whose blood all Narnia was saved."[24] There is more than a hint here that the Islamic martyr who dies killing himself and others is not to be equated with the Christian martyr who follows Christ's example by dying in faithful but nonviolent proclamation of the gospel.

While some are taken in by the deception of "Tashlan," there is an inner circle of apostates who believe in neither Aslan nor Tash. Ginger the cat discerns the unbelief in Shift's Calormene associate, Rishda Tarkaan, and has a secret meeting to confirm that what it really means to identify Aslan and Tash is "that there's no such person as either."[25] Behind the show of inclusive piety there is a cynical desire to use a false civil religion as an opiate for the masses, controlling their behavior by drugging them with an empty hope. Ginger the cat is horrified to learn that Tash is a real but demonic power summoned to the stable in unbelief by Rishda Tarkaan. Ginger is punished for his apostasy by reverting to a dumb cat, bereft of language, as Aslan had long ago warned would happen.[26] Likewise, Rishda Tarkaan is astonished when Tash devours Shift[27] and tries in vain to make up for his unbelief by throwing Narnians into the stable as sacrifices to Tash.[28] In the end, more and more people end up in the stable and encounter the transcendent, either in the frightful form of Tash who claims Rishda Tarkaan as his prey,[29] or in the beautiful form of Aslan. But the dwarfs experience neither. They have so blinded themselves to the transcendent that they cannot see it in front of their faces.

Refusing to Be Taken In

When Tirian is freed by Jill Pole and Eustace, they take Puzzle the donkey to expose the ape's deception. But when the dwarfs see that they have been taken in by a false Aslan, they respond not with the joy of liberation but with a sullen refusal to believe in the true Aslan: "We've been fooled once and we're not going to be fooled again."[30]

THERE IS NO WAY THAT THE TERRIBLE GOD TASH WHO FED ON THE BLOOD OF HIS PEOPLE COULD POSSIBLY BE THE SAME AS THE GOOD LION BY WHOSE BLOOD ALL NARNIA WAS SAVED.

TASH

Tirian is horrified to learn that "one of the results of an Ape's setting up a false Aslan would be to stop people believing in the real one."[31]

When the dwarfs are thrown by the Calormenes into the stable, their experience is stunningly different from that of the believing Narnians. The latter can see blue sky and beautiful countryside, but the dwarfs' refusal to be "taken in," means they can no longer believe what is given in their immediate experience. For believers there is a whole world inside the stable that is bigger than the stable itself, just as Narnia is much bigger than a wardrobe. Lucy grasps the Christian significance: "In our world too, a stable once had something in it that was bigger than our whole world."[32] Meanwhile the dwarfs are closed to the transcendent and can see only a "pitch-black, poky, smelly little hole of a stable,"[33] like an ordinary dark wardrobe with a wooden back and mothballs. When offered flowers, they are interpreted as stable litter. Then Aslan appears, and provides a great banquet, but like those who excuse themselves in the parable (Luke 14:15–24), the dwarfs do not appreciate the gift: "They thought they were eating and drinking only the sort of things you might find in a stable."[34] Following the kind of skepticism encouraged by the witch of Underland, the dwarfs reduce miraculous gifts to mundane matter.

We learn that Christ gives us the choice to disbelieve in his free offer of grace. Although Aslan reaches out in love, the dwarfs have so hardened themselves in unbelief that they cannot trust the offer. Aslan explains: "They will not let us help them. They have chosen cunning instead of belief. Their prison is only in their own minds, yet they are in that prison; and so afraid of being taken in that they cannot be taken out."[35]

THE JOYOUS REUNION OF BELIEVERS IN THE NEW NARNIA AND THE TRAGIC SELF-CONDEMNATION OF UNBELIEVERS ARE A POINTED REMINDER THAT BELIEFS HAVE NOT ONLY TEMPORAL BUT ETERNAL CONSEQUENCES.

The joyous reunion of believers in the new Narnia and the tragic self-condemnation of unbelievers are a pointed reminder that beliefs have not only temporal but eternal consequences. Modern secularism may undermine imagination and ethics in this life, but it also fosters unbelief that may condemn a person eternally. A syncretic civil religion may seem to help people get along better in this life, but it may also lead people away from their true Savior. A wardrobe that remains closed to transcendence, or one that opens but discovers only doctrinal indifferentism and syncretism, may morph into the pitch-black hole of a self-imposed hell. But a wardrobe that opens to the transcendent incarnate that is Christ Jesus born in a stable is a portal to paradise.

ENDNOTES:

1. C. S. Lewis, *The Lion, the Witch and the Wardrobe* (New York: Harper Trophy, 1994), 48.
2. Ibid., 25.
3. Ibid., 48.
4. C. S. Lewis, *Prince Caspian* (New York: Harper Trophy, 1994), 44.
5. Ibid., 199.
6. Ibid., 200.
7. C. S. Lewis, "Miracles" in Walter Hooper, ed., *God in the Dock* (Grand Rapids, Mich.: William B. Eerdmans, 1970), 25–37.
8. Ibid., 25.
9. Lewis uses this term in *The Abolition of Man* (New York: Macmillan, 1955). It is a reference to Plato's three-part model of the soul in which the head represents the reason; the belly, the appetite; and the chest, the seat of moral value.
10. C. S. Lewis, *The Voyage of the Dawn Treader* (New York: Harper Trophy, 1994), 87.
11. Ibid., 11.
12. C. S. Lewis, *The Silver Chair* (New York: Harper Trophy, 1994), 3.
13. Ibid., 7.
14. Ibid., 242.
15. Lewis, *Prince Caspian*, 51.
16. Lewis, *The Silver Chair*, 167.
17. Ibid., 178.
18. Ibid., 180.
19. Ibid., 182.
20. C. S. Lewis, *The Horse and His Boy* (New York: Harper Trophy, 1994), 199.
21. Ibid., 200.
22. Ibid., 201.
23. C. S. Lewis, *The Last Battle* (New York: Harper Trophy, 1994), 38–39.
24. Ibid., 40.
25. Ibid., 89.
26. Ibid., 124.
27. Ibid., 130.
28. Ibid., 134.
29. Ibid., 150.
30. Ibid., 82.
31. Ibid., 84.
32. Ibid., 161.
33. Ibid., 165.
34. Ibid., 168.
35. Ibid., 169.

*N*arnia reminds us that an essential part of the longing for paradise in the future is a healing of the old wound between man and beast. —Andrew Cuneo

FLEDGE

10

"His Speech Has Gone Out into All Lands": The Talking Beasts of Narnia

Andrew Cuneo

Andrew Cuneo is an assistant professor of English literature at Hillsdale College. He completed his master's and doctoral work at Merton College, Oxford University. While most of his work there concerned the unpublished letters of C. S. Lewis, he also saw several lampposts that looked a good deal like what Lucy saw—and a white stag.

I have always been charmed by the story of C. S. Lewis feeding bread dipped in port to the deer that roamed his college grounds. There are still deer at Magdalen College; in fact, there is still a white stag there, though perhaps no one feeds him such unusual winter food. The story indicates an author with a humorous sensibility toward the animal world. His household, The Kilns, with its long sequence of dogs and cats and war-stranded children was itself a menagerie of animals and people whom Lewis dutifully tended—even a random hedgehog who once wandered in for a saucer of milk. This is the Old Professor who gave us Narnia, a real Professor Kirk in an actual country home. But I doubt whether the animals actually spoke to him; indeed, what strikes me about the fairy-tale tradition in which C. S. Lewis writes The Chronicles of Narnia is the presence of *talking* beasts.

At the outset, even the four Pevensie children and a frightful white witch are not as unusual as the fact that, in Narnia, the animals speak. The richness of narrative color in Narnia comes from more than the snow, the lampposts, and the Turkish delight; it comes from the first "good gracious me!" of Mr. Tumnus, the faun who greets little Lucy. Lucy takes it all in without a flicker of surprise—along with a brown egg, sardines, and some buttered toast. She has the faith of a small child; she accepts the magic that gives to Narnian animals the gift of speech.

Mr. Tumnus

This is more than just high storytelling, though; there is a deep theological importance in the ability of animals to speak. We are all, as Lewis reminds us in *Mere Christianity*, filled with a longing for the original holiness of Eden. We all too, he adds, long for paradise in the future. Narnia reminds us that an essential part of that longing is a healing of the old wound between man and beast. Was it not through a talking beast, the serpent, that temptation first entered the world? Ever since then, sin has separated man from God, and man from creation—including its animals. Sin has sundered man from God, the angels, the beasts, and even the inanimate world about him.

> WE ARE ALL FILLED WITH A LONGING FOR THE ORIGINAL HOLINESS OF EDEN.—C. S. LEWIS

The world of Narnia is not free from these effects of the fall. But there is hope, given in certain kinds of literature. J. R. R. Tolkien comments on this hope with his usual insight in his essay "On Fairy Stories." Fairy tales, in his view, satisfy "the desire of men to hold communion with other living things."[1] This remark naturally presupposes an absence of communion in our present state. For most of us, serpents do not tempt, donkeys do not rebuke their masters (Num. 22:28), and badgers do not offer us tea. "Living things," Tolkien adds, means more than dwarfs, fauns, and elves. He includes inanimate nature, too. We desire a kind of communion with *all* created things, animate and inanimate. Stones, rivers, birds, trees: Tolkien notes that fairy tales give speech to all these things. (We are thus not far from Tolkien's creation of the Ents, the talking trees, in *The Lord of the Rings*. How amusing and revealing are C. S. Lewis's recollections of Tolkien as a man who would actually embrace the trees.

> FAIRY TALES SATISFY THE DESIRE OF MEN TO HOLD COMMUNION WITH OTHER LIVING THINGS.
> —J. R. R. TOLKIEN

WILLOW DRYAD

How rich that Tolkein would base his Entish leader Treebeard on Lewis.) In sum, man desires to be in communion with the whole world; he looks for right relationship with all of God's creation.[2] Fairy tales in part reflect that desire.

In the great tradition of St. Francis of Assisi in the West or St. Anthony of Egypt in the East, C. S. Lewis gives us a world of nature where we may relate rightly to God. The world is, to borrow from the poet Gerard Manley Hopkins, charged with the grandeur of God. Hopkins himself merely echoes the psalmist in Psalm 19 who writes that the heavens declare God's glory. How much more, in their own way, do the creatures of the sea and the creatures of the land? To understand and love them is one of the chief ways one understands and loves him. God has us love him (whom we cannot see) by way of the things we can see: nature and neighbor alike. Indeed, it is by loving all that is in the world, forest and beast and neighbor, that one loves his Maker.

Furthermore, one comes to know mankind a little bit better by his furred and feathered friends. C. S. Lewis appreciated how one knows the greater (man) by the lesser (animals) in the created world. That is, by understanding the talking animals in fairy stories, one understands man, another "talking animal," in ordinary life. In his essay

GLIMFEATHER

ONE COMES TO KNOW MANKIND A LITTLE BETTER BY HIS FURRED AND FEATHERED FRIENDS.

"On Three Ways of Writing for Children," Lewis remarks that it is precisely through animals acting humanly that one sees all the varieties of human psychology and character. The reader who has met Mr. Toad in *The Wind in the Willows*, for instance, acquires a firsthand knowledge of the type of man who is ever pursuing and ever disappointed by the shiny and the

MR. & MRS. BEAVER

new. In fact, such a man is visiting my house next week. All the varieties of the human soul take on life and texture in the talking beasts of children's stories.

Such beasts can also make an important moral point. Speech is what makes an animal more than just a beast in Narnia; it makes the animals like Aslan himself. Frighteningly, this gift of likeness to Aslan can be lost. Lewis describes this potential when Narnia itself is sung into being by Aslan in *The Magician's Nephew*. In this sixth book of The Chronicles, Aslan creates some beasts for love, speech, and thought, but not all. Those with speech are to cherish those animals without speech and, more significantly, can lose their own abilities if they behave like the speechless animals. They are *given* speech by Aslan; it can be taken away. The noble animals of Narnia display this potential for loss of speech in *The Last Battle*. Several animals lose their intelligence by serving the false god Tash and descend down to the level of ordinary, mute beasts.

What Lewis here indicates with the animals also applies to human beings, for humans also have the capacity to lose their divinely given dignity and descend into beastliness. What follows is a picture of human nature that Lewis keenly preserved and explained in many of his books. Ever present in man are his lower appetites, his nature that he shares with the beasts; also ever present are his higher faculties, his intelligence and reason that he shares with the angels. Therein lies the peril for reason: usurpation by the appetites. The ancient Greek myths, for instance, portray these two dimensions in man by their symbolic creature, the centaur: a half-horse, half-man hybrid.

WITH THE ABUSE OF REASON, ACCORDING TO THE GREEKS (AND LEWIS), MAN CAN FALL INTO THE STATE OF THE BEAST.

CENTAUR

LEWIS APPROVES OF THE GREEK CONCEPTION OF MAN AS **ANIMAL RATIONALE,** MAN THE RATIONAL ANIMAL. FOR IT IS PARTLY BY OUR REASON AND SPEECH, OUR **LOGOS,** THAT WE REFLECT THE DIVINE **LOGOS.**

With the abuse of reason, according to the Greeks (and Lewis), man can fall into the state of the beast. He can, if you will, devolve. For this reason Lewis approves of the Greek conception of man as *animal rationale*, man the rational animal. For it is partly by our reason and speech, our *logos*, that we reflect the divine *Logos*.

Thus, the loss of speech is particularly ominous in Narnia. Here as ever, the magic of the white witch differs so greatly from the magic of Aslan. Whereas Aslan confers speech upon the simple animals, the white witch either distorts it (e.g., the snapping of Fenris Ulf) or takes it away altogether. She uses her most powerful weapon, her wand, to turn the animals of Narnia into stone: lions, squirrels, foxes, even Mr. Tumnus. Stone deaf, stone mute, all with the wave of a wand. Aslan, conversely, is a life- and speech-giving lord. He breathes upon the stone statues in Jadis's castle, and the stone turns into flesh. What he does with stone he can also do with the seasons. The thaw, the glorious thaw that Aslan begins in Narnia, is simply his doing on a large scale what he does on a smaller scale with the stone statues. New life is given to the animals and new life, a real spring, is given to Narnia.

No one can afterwards mistake the speech of the Narnian animals once they are unstoned anymore than the white witch can

WHAT ASLAN DOES WITH STONE HE CAN ALSO DO WITH THE SEASONS. NEW LIFE IS GIVEN TO THE ANIMALS AND NEW LIFE, A REAL SPRING, IS GIVEN TO NARNIA.

mistake the hum of the bumblebee meaning spring. The witch's prison of statues turns into a boisterous zoo; the wintry white of her courtyard comes back into full color; "and instead of the deadly silence, the place rang with the sound of happy roarings, brayings, yelpings, barkings, squealings, cooings, neighings, stampings, shouts, hurrahs, songs, and laughter."[3] Lewis here gives a full concert of animals at their most voluble; he follows it with the overwhelming roar of Aslan. What is most interesting is how for those who love Aslan, the speech is intelligible; for those who follow the witch, it is cacophony. One cannot forget Uncle Andrew in *The Magician's Nephew* who hears the speech of Aslan as only a roar and the talk of a bulldog as only a growl.

One must have "ears to hear" even in Narnia. More often than not, it is the children and not the adults who have them.

As a young child, I myself used to love imagining the animals about me as able to speak. It must have been partially due to Narnia. As incorrect as I may have been in attributing speech to the beasts in the real world, there is, I trust, a natural impulse behind the activity. Part of the joy of fairy tales is that they allow the whole world to cry out in praise of its Creator. From Rumblebuffin down to Reepicheep, Aslan has redeemed the entire creation, and those redeemed will talk about it. In closing, I do not think Lewis is far from what is repeated so often in Genesis in a crucial phrase. Three of the most important, if simple, words in the creation account of Genesis are "And God *said*"; God's speech, so the early Christian fathers tell us, lies in the heart of all that is. When Adam names the animals, he listens, as it were, to the names God has placed within them. The divine Word hides a little word in all that he makes. Adam's task is to listen to the divine speech in the whole of creation. He never knows what he might hear; for the Lord who spoke all things into existence has the power to make all things in existence speak.

FROM RUMBLEBUFFIN DOWN TO REEPICEEP, ASLAN HAS REDEEMED THE ENTIRE CREATION, AND THOSE REDEEMED WILL TALK ABOUT IT.

REEPICEEP

Endnotes:

1. J. R. R. Tolkien, "On Fairy Stories" in *Tree and Leaf* (London: Unwin Hyman, 1988), 19.

2. Lewis has filled *The Lion, the Witch and the Wardrobe* with examples of restored human/animal inter-action. At a crucial moment, it is a simple robin red-breast who leads the Pevensie children to Mr. and Mrs. Beaver. The bird is deliberately silent, but he *understands* what the children are saying and acts accordingly. One also remembers the mice who nibble through Aslan's bonds on the stone table and are consequently rewarded with speech. Even the white stag at the end of the book is pursued, not hunted for the kill. Some talking creatures are perilous, though. Mr. and Mrs. Beaver themselves fear the trees because they might betray the followers of Aslan to the white witch, and virtually no wolf in Narnia can be trusted.

3. C. S. Lewis, *The Lion, the Witch and the Wardrobe* (New York: Macmillan, 1998), 137.

The end of all things is near; therefore ... be hospitable.
—1 Peter 4:7, 9

THE BEAVERS FEED THE CHILDREN

11

FOOD FOR THE SOUL: EATING IN NARNIA

WAYNE MARTINDALE AND KATHRYN WELCH

Wayne Martindale is professor of English at Wheaton College, Illinois; author of the recently published *Beyond the Shadowlands: C. S. Lewis on Heaven and Hell*; and coeditor of *The Quotable Lewis*. Kathryn Welch is a Wheaton College student who plans to attend law school on the west coast.

Generations of readers hungry for the truth have found food for their souls in Lewis's Chronicles of Narnia. Fittingly, of all the image patterns weaving in and out of the Narnia books, eating ranks among the most striking. From the first book to the last, as well as in many of Lewis's other works, we are never long without food. Lewis invites us to partake of not only the domestic meal but also the kingly feast. He tantalizes our taste buds with vividly described spreads of food but also gives us many symbolic scenes ranging from devouring demons to sacramental moments echoing the Lord's Supper, addressing the gamut

> THE "ORIGINAL" SIN IS NOT PRIMARILY THAT MAN HAS "DISOBEYED" GOD; THE SIN IS THAT HE CEASED TO BE HUNGRY FOR GOD AND GOD ALONE.
>
> —C. S. LEWIS

of spiritual significance. Spiritually, imaginatively, and intellectually, all are invited to the high table: Narnia is food for the soul.

To dwell on the metaphor for a moment, Lewis's first gift is often to whet our appetites for spiritual nourishment. David Fagerberg ponders, "Why are we not naturally conformed to God's love? Our appetites have been misdirected, leading us to

believe that there is a contradiction between God's glory and our own happiness, that we cannot submit our lives to God and still have what we really want. The 'original' sin is not primarily that man has 'disobeyed' God; the sin is that he ceased to be hungry for God and God alone."[1] Here at once we have the root of human sin, its consequence in our dysfunctional relation to God, and, serendipitously, in the word "hungry" an entrée into one of Lewis's major metaphors for the spiritual life.

As humans, we need food—and the right food; we can't eat just anything. Only certain plants and animals constitute what we know to be "people food." In *The Magician's Nephew*, Digory and Polly look at each other in dismay when their horse, Fledge, enthusiastically suggests that they satiate their hunger with mouthfuls of grass. "But we can't eat grass," Digory insists.[2] It's a simple but crucial point. Our bodies require specific nutrients, as is often reflected by our cravings. Likewise, we were created to be sustained by only certain spiritual food. But occasionally we need to be reminded, "No, that's not for eating." Good food is available, but not all food is good. What we eat can spell the difference between growth and stagnation or even life and death. One of the most moving uses of food as a metaphor for spiritual nourishment comes in *The Problem of Pain*. "God is the only good of all creatures; . . . that there ever could be any other good, is an atheistic dream. . . . God gives us what He has, not what He has not: He gives the happiness that there is, not the happiness that is not. To be God—to be like God and to share His goodness in creaturely response—to be miserable—these are the only three alternatives. If we will not learn to eat the only food that the universe grows—the only food that any possible universe ever can grow—then we must starve eternally."[3]

GOD IS THE ONLY GOOD OF ALL CREATURES; . . . THAT THERE EVER COULD BE ANY OTHER GOOD, IS AN ATHEISTIC DREAM.

—C. S. LEWIS, THE PROBLEM OF PAIN

Our souls must be nourished by the bread of heaven.

The fact of human hunger is inescapable and is often the occasion of God's miraculous provision. When the Pevensie children are again whisked unsuspectingly off to Narnia in *Prince Caspian*, the first order of business is to provide for their basic needs of food and water. Susan insightfully observes, "I suppose we'll have to make some plans. We shall want something to eat before long."[4] In his divine goodness God provides for their hunger. The children find a freshwater pool and apple trees—apple trees amidst the now ancient ruins of Cair Paravel where they had once feasted as royalty. Aslan, while providing for their needs, was intentionally leading them to a place prophetic of Narnia's return to right rule. Returning to the plight of Digory and Polly, we find the youngsters resting in the assurance that Aslan will supply them with food. Polly does indeed find some toffee in her pocket, but it's hardly enough to sustain them through their journey. They plant a piece, in faith, hoping to repeat the miracle of the lamppost grown from an iron bar. Sure enough, they awake the following morning to the sight of a toffee tree. The supply of "daily bread" is occasion enough for the miraculous as God supplies the needs he created us with, needs which demonstrate our dependence on him.

Lewis's application of eating imagery ranges from the ordinary and natural to the extraordinary and supernatural. As we have seen in these first examples, he deals extensively with food and drink realistically as an important part of everyday life. It is crucial not to overlook the realm of the ordinary, where we should not be surprised to find deep significance from a man who cherished routine and championed domesticity. What to most would be ordinary is to Lewis extraordinary: "There are no ordinary people," he says so memorably in "The Weight of Glory," "you have never talked to a mere mortal."[5] His sense of God's immanence extends to all creation and all human acts, asserting that "there is no neutral ground in the universe: every square inch, every split second, is claimed by God and counterclaimed by Satan."[6] The same is true of such mundane human activity as making and eating meals and entertaining guests.

In fact, such domestic activities are, in Lewis's view, the very thing governments exist to protect, as he maintains in *Mere Christianity*: "The State exists simply to promote and to protect the ordinary happiness of human beings in this life. A husband and wife chatting over a fire, a couple of friends having a game of darts in a pub, a man reading a book in his own room or digging in his own garden—that is what the State is there for."

If they are not aspiring to this end, Lewis continues, all of the laws and institutions of the State are "a waste of time."[7] Lewis held quiet domesticity in such high esteem that it effectively legitimizes the state as its protector. One such encounter with the domestic comes early on in *The Lion, the Witch and the Wardrobe.* Mr. and Mrs. Beaver host the Pevensie children in their home and generously spread before them a home-cooked meal.

The meal is not simply filler. Not only does it provide a touch of realism; it espouses the value of hospitality. Each aspect of the scene, including Mr. Beaver's fetching of the fresh fish, the generous supply of butter, Mrs. Beaver's preparing of the sticky marmalade roll, the special allotment of milk for the children, and the intimate nature of the group sitting on wooden stools around a common table demonstrates the warmth and welcome inherent in hospitality. Clearly it is a grace. Hospitality certainly wasn't a foreign concept to Lewis, who treasured the ancient epics, reading them in the original languages. Homer's writings, for example, are saturated with the practice of hospitality.

Upon the appearance of a stranger, the host must meet the guest's need for food, a bath, oil for the body, and rest before inquiring about the visitor's business. Such caretaking was necessary for survival in ancient travels. The prospect of a stranger being in actuality a god or goddess in disguise added extra incentive.

Biblical injunctions to hospitality provide a parallel in the caution that we may be entertaining angels unaware (Heb. 13:2). The apostle Peter gives an even more stunning context, instructing followers of Christ on how to live, knowing that "the heavens will pass away with a roar, and the heavenly bodies will be burned up and dissolved" (2 Pet. 3:10 ESV): "The end of all things is near; therefore . . . be hospitable." (1 Pet. 4:7, 9). Since hospitality to friends and strangers ranks as a high virtue in both the biblical and classical sources Lewis esteemed, it does not surprise us to find Lewis emphasizing them in The Chronicles of Narnia. The domestic scene at Mr. and Mrs. Beaver's, which must soon be lost in the battle with usurping evil, is among the very things to be recovered by the victory—both in Narnia and on earth. The peace and intimacy of the shared meal has been threatened by forces of evil and must therefore be reclaimed in the name of the king.

NOT ONLY DOES THE BEAVER'S MEAL PROVIDE A TOUCH OF REALISM; IT ESPOUSES THE VALUE OF HOSPITALITY.

Eating in Narnia often assumes a deeper theological significance, as illustrated in the plight of young Edmund in *The Lion, the Witch and the Wardrobe*. Edmund, as yet the very type of the spiteful and emotionally bullying older brother, has come into Narnia with egg on his face. Lucy is right; he is wrong. Enter Jadis, the white witch, with an offer he can't refuse. First, here's a chance to lord it over the others by becoming king of Narnia, knowing a secret they don't know, and tapping a power source unavailable to them. The apparent earnest on this promise is the magical appearance of his first wish, which is for the candy called Turkish delight—not for nourishment but for pleasure. Edmund assumes, since the witch came through on the Turkish delight, that she will come through on her promise to make him king. This is a case of wishful thinking, the sort that we all engage in when rationalizing some attractive indulgence we know deep down is sin.

It is no mere coincidence that, as with Adam and Eve, sin often takes the form of eating in The Chronicles. Here, abandoned to the dictates of his stomach, Edmund falls prey to the sin of gluttony. Gerard Reed remarks that "gluttony is a deadly sin because it so easily leads us to exchange essentially good things for things that superficially taste good."[8] Edmund is later unable to appreciate the simple fare provided by the Beavers; rather, he fantasizes about Turkish delight. Gluttony necessarily excludes gratitude—the former wholly concerned with the filling of self; the latter centered on the subordination of self. Consequently gluttony focuses on the gift rather than the giver. Edmund's gorging on sweets contrasts starkly with the selfless hospitality of the Beavers and the other Pevensie children's enjoyment of their food and company. Edmund never gets enough, which is always the way with sin—it never satisfies—and, on top of that, it ruins his appetite for healthy food. So obsessed does Edmund become with the memory of Turkish delight that he is impelled to slip away from the small band at supper and seek out the white witch. Jadis recognizes the children as a threat to her claim on Narnia, so she entices this "son of Adam" by appealing to his baser nature. Like his original, Edmund is not long in Narnia before he succumbs to the tempter. Lulled into a fantasy world of endless Turkish delight and kingly command, Edmund unwittingly conspires to bring about even his own ruin.

GLUTTONY IS A DEADLY SIN BECAUSE IT SO EASILY LEADS US TO EXCHANGE ESSENTIALLY GOOD THINGS FOR THINGS THAT SUPERFICIALLY TASTE GOOD.

—GERARD REED

EDMUND

Edmund's indulgence of his appetite to a sinful degree leads him to betray his friends and family.

That gluttony is a serious sin with serious consequences we need not doubt, and Edmund is not the only one to learn this lesson. The demon Screwtape, who knows it from the other side, berates his nephew Wormwood in *The Screwtape Letters* upon the latter's dismissal of gluttony as inconsequential. Screwtape explains that desensitizing humans to gluttony's damning potential is one of Satan's greatest advances. In Screwtape's hands the temptation is far more subtle, and we learn that it is possible not only to partake of the wrong foods but to partake of food wrongly. Reed explains, "Too often limited to discussions of specific acts—overeating or drunkenness—gluttony actually refers to the abuse of good things. It's more an attitude than an act, more evident in the priorities by which we live than the portions of meat and potatoes we place on our plates."[9] Gluttony is a deeply rooted sin that, while exercised on the physical level, ultimately involves the heart.

The church has traditionally understood the "vice of gluttony" as the act of eating "hastily, sumptuously, too much, greedily, daintily."[10] Traditionally, gluttony doesn't necessarily presuppose the consumption of large portions of food. *The Screwtape Letters*

offers a poignant example of what Lewis termed "gluttony of Delicacy, not gluttony of Excess." We make the acquaintance of a woman gluttonous in her demands on people, always wanting something other than what is offered, just a little, of course, if it is not too much trouble—but it always is. She loudly insists that her food be prepared in just such a manner as she indicates. Lewis observes that, as is true of all gluttons, this woman's "belly now dominates her whole life."[11] Accordingly, gluttony is a sin that dictates lifestyle and mind-set alike. The main focus is self and fulfilling of selfish desires.

Eustace Scrubb, in *The Voyage of the Dawn Treader* and in one of the most dramatic episodes of The Chronicles, awakes to find himself in the form of a dragon. The sin of greed is at the root of his metamorphosis; and greed, of course, is rooted in self. He emerges from the dragon cave in search of food and, finding a dragon carcass nearby, devours it. He is, in fact, eating a fellow dragon in the same way that the demons (followers of "that old serpent, the Devil") see even one another as food. There is, then, some truth to the saying that "you are what you eat." Reed aptly observes that "whatever we ingest—physically, intellectually, or spiritually—we digest."[12] In the most literal sense possible, Eustace becomes the sin that he indulges.

EUSTACE AWAKES TO FIND HIMSELF IN THE FORM OF A DRAGON . . . THE SIN OF GREED IS AT THE ROOT OF HIS METAMORPHOSIS.

Eustace has a dragonish greed that lures him to desert his tried shipmates and then enter a dragon's cave where he finds and dons a gold bracelet, then becomes a dragon. His greedy, dragonish thoughts precipitate his transformation into a dragon, even to the point of eating dragon's food—other dragons.

The Silver Chair, which recounts the travels of Eustace Scrubb, Jill Pole, and Puddleglum the Marshwiggle, explores the danger of selfishly focusing on personal comfort, feasting when they should be fasting. Having sought shelter at the castle of Harfang, home to a family of giants, the trio of Narnians is hosted generously. What would be a virtue in a different setting with different motives is here a treacherous trap. The queen orders comforts to be supplied to her guests, including a lavish meal and toys. One giant whispers to the weepy Jill, "Don't cry, little girl, or you won't be good for anything when the feast comes."[13] Lulled in the lap of luxury, Jill readily yields to sleep in her soft bed. She forgets Aslan's directive to daily repeat the "signs." The danger of gluttony in this case is much more subtle and ironic: the Narnians are intended to *be* the feast! Only Aslan's dramatic appearance to Jill enables the Narnians to escape with their lives. As the episode at Harfang illustrates, we must take not only the right food but at the right time and in the right circumstances.

As in the book of Revelation, Aslan brings joy and feasting, a common motif in Narnia, when he finishes some great work. It draws on the chivalric elements that thread through the stories and parallel Jesus' ministry. On more than one occasion, Jesus fed multitudes miraculously, and he promises the grandest feast of all when he gathers us in heaven for the wedding feast of the Lamb. Feasting is associated both with life, as a necessity, and with joyful celebration in peace and plenty. Still there is a degree of trust involved in feasting: you must trust the host. We read that Ramandu's feast in *The Voyage of the Dawn Treader* is "such a banquet as had never been seen." However, the comrades are reluctant to taste the spread because it seems that magic is afoot.

As in the Book of Revelation, Aslan brings JOY and FEASTING, a common motif in Narnia, when he finishes some great work.

Edmund inquires of the young woman who invites them to eat how they can know it's safe. Her reply is simply, "You can't know. . . . You can only believe—or not."[14] The party is aware that the table is set and sustained by Aslan's decree, but they are faced with risk regardless. Implicit here is the truth that eating at God's table requires an element of trust.

This feast is appropriately situated in the chapter entitled "The Beginning of the End of the World." This reminds us that the destination of the *Dawn Treader* is Aslan's country. Couched in sacramental imagery and classical elements of hospitality, Ramandu's table serves a dual purpose. First, it refreshes the weary travelers on the way to their true destination. Food is provided to give strength and allow the journey to continue. Second, it prepares the travelers for what is to come. This daily-renewed feast gives a foretaste of what lies at the end of the world for those who are seeking it.

As they sail nearer to Aslan's country, references to Christ and our heavenly home accumulate quickly. Reepicheep discovers that the water is sweet! Caspian describes the phenomenon with synesthesia, using the terms of one sense experience to describe another: "It—it's like light more than anything else."[15] The water is also filling, such that the Narnians no longer have to eat. This echoes Jesus' words to the woman at the well that one drinking of the water he gives never will thirst again. Then at the world's end the children see a lamb cooking fish on the shore, a lamb that turns into Aslan the lion. This episode is meant to recall Jesus' cooking fish for his disciples, which he eats to prove that he has risen from the dead. His appearance as lamb reminds that he is the Lamb of God, the perfect sacrifice for our sins.

Like the Narnians at Ramandu's table, Jill Pole struggles with trust as a necessity for obtaining living water in *The Silver Chair*. She is intensely thirsty, but the lion Aslan is between her and the stream. When Jill prevails upon him to "go away" so she can drink without perceived threat, Aslan responds with a low growl of disapproval. Since he won't move, Jill tries to exact assurances from him:

> "Will you promise not to——do anything to me, if I do come?" said Jill.
>
> "I make no promise," said the Lion. Jill was so thirsty now that, without noticing it, she had come a step nearer.
>
> "Do you eat girls?" she said.
>
> "I have swallowed up girls and boys, women and men, kings and emperors, cities and realms," said the Lion. It didn't say this as if it were boasting, nor as if it were sorry, nor as if it were angry. It just said it.
>
> "I daren't come and drink," said Jill.
>
> "Then you will die of thirst," said the Lion.
>
> "Oh dear!" said Jill, coming another step nearer. "I suppose I must go and look for another stream then."
>
> "There is no other stream," said the Lion.[16]

This passage is loaded with theological significance and biblical echoes. Most immediately it evokes the account in John 4 of Jesus with a Samaritan woman at a well. Jesus implies, as he straightforwardly claims elsewhere, that he is the living water and anyone who drinks this water "will never be thirsty forever" (John 4:14 ESV). When Jill Pole decides she must risk all and drink from the stream, she finds it "the most refreshing water she had ever tasted" and that "you didn't need to drink much of it, for it quenched your thirst at once."[17] The drinking in both events also suggests Holy Communion, in which we drink of Jesus.

And Lewis often uses the metaphors of eating and drinking to suggest total commitment and hence total blessing. First the total necessity: "He claims all because He is love and must bless. He cannot bless us unless He has us. . . . Therefore, in love He claims all. There is no bargaining with Him."[18]

In *The Horse and His Boy*, Bree the Narnian-talking war horse, like most of us, likes to be in charge and has his full quotient of pride and must, predictably, be humbled. Like Jill he wants to command his own destiny and is fearful of Aslan. Unlike either of these two, Hwin, a Narnian mare, is so trusting, so simply in love with Aslan, that she wholly submits in this poignantly metaphorical language (we read it as metaphor, but she really means it): "Please, you're so beautiful. You may eat me if you like. I'd sooner be eaten by you than fed by anyone else."[19] This contrasts with Jill's fear of being eaten by Aslan and with eating as a selfish act of dominance, as in *The Screwtape Letters* with Screwtape threatening to consume Wormwood, the demons threatening to dine on every human they can dupe, and Tash gobbling up Shift in *The Last Battle*. Hwin's submission to be eaten by Aslan is a desire to be consumed by him, a metaphor for complete union, which is our heart's deepest desire, the consummation of all desires. It contrasts directly with hell's aim, which is to consume and enlarge the self at others' expense. Screwtape, in his "Toast," views all humans won to hell as food. Hwin's submission to be eaten by Aslan overflows with love and trust; Screwtape's with hatred, double cross, and the gluttony of the persistently asserted self.

It is evident by this point that we have transitioned from the ordinary to the extraordinary: from the Beavers' mealtime hospitality to miraculous provisions at Ramandu's table; from raw dragon, as Eustace feeds upon his scaly counterpart, to devouring demons contrasted by the total submission of Hwin, as she literally offers herself to be eaten by Aslan. Finally we have seen episodes of eating rich with biblical allusion to Christ, from his earthly use of food

to teach about himself and his kingdom to the communion meal, all with overtones of the supernatural. We have seen that every example of eating in The Chronicles, including the most ordinary, is imbued with spiritual significance of the highest degree.

We feed on the spoiled fruits of sin when we are self-centered, but our palates are ultimately satisfied by the bread of heaven and water of life when we yield ourselves to God to taste of him and see that he is good (Ps. 34:8). Thus, a dichotomy is established: the unrighteous live to eat, while the righteous eat to live. The biblical model of eating, as embodied perfectly in the person of Jesus Christ, engenders an entirely self-sacrificial devotion to God. Shortly after

his conversation with the woman at the well, Jesus' disciples join him, urging him to eat something. "But he said to them, 'I have food to eat that you do not know about.'" Bewildered, the disciples wonder if someone could have brought him food. "Jesus said to them, 'My food is to do the will of him who sent me and to accomplish his work'" (John 4:32, 34 ESV). This is a picture of ultimate communion, where life is totally Christ centered and therefore food in and of itself. The feasting is continuous as long as we are hungry for God.

Lewis says the "joys of Heaven are, for most of us in our present condition, 'an acquired taste'—and certain ways of life may render the taste impossible of

WE FEED ON THE SPOILED FRUITS OF SIN WHEN WE ARE SELF-CENTERED, BUT OUR PALATES ARE ULTIMATLEY SATISFIED BY THE BREAD OF HEAVEN AND WATER OF LIFE WHEN WE YIELD OURSELVES TO GOD TO TASTE OF HIM AND SEE THAT HE IS GOOD.

acquisition."[20] This truth is all too apparent in *The Last Battle*. The dwarfs are utterly incapable of appreciating the feast spread before them by Aslan. They mistake the pies and meats for hay and turnips, and each one suspecting that his neighbor has received a better dish than he, they begin to brawl. Their prideful proclamation, "The dwarfs are for the dwarfs," amply summarizes their constriction into the self.[21] The bread of heaven is an acquired taste. We don't have all the time in the world to acquire that taste. We have only our time in the world. In Jesus, the feast is before us, and all are invited. Let us heed Aslan's warning, for "there is no other."

ENDNOTES:

1. David W. Fagerberg, "Between Heaven and Earth: C. S. Lewis on Asceticism and Holiness," *Touchstone* 17, no. 3 (April 2004): 30–35. See page 31.
2. C. S. Lewis, *The Magician's Nephew* (New York: HarperCollins, 1994), 178.
3. C. S. Lewis, *The Problem of Pain* (New York: Macmillan, 1962), 54.
4. C. S. Lewis, *Prince Caspian* (New York: HarperCollins, 1994), 4.
5. C. S. Lewis, "The Weight of Glory" in *The Weight of Glory and Other Addresses* (New York: Simon & Schuster, 1996), 39.
6. Ibid., 33.
7. C. S. Lewis, *Mere Christianity* (New York: Macmillan, 1960), 169.
8. Gerard Reed, *C. S. Lewis Explores Vice and Virtue* (Kansas City: Beacon Hill Press of Kansas City, 2001), 63.
9. C. S. Lewis, *The Screwtape Letters* (New York: Simon & Schuster, 1996), 67.
10. Reed, *C. S. Lewis Explores Vice and Virtue*, 62–63.
11. Ibid., 68.
12. Ibid., 62.
13. C. S. Lewis, *The Silver Chair* (New York: HarperCollins, 1994), 115.
14. C. S. Lewis, *The Voyage of the Dawn Treader* (New York: HarperCollins, 1994), 217.
15. Ibid., 248.
16. Lewis, *The Silver Chair*, 21.
17. Ibid., 21.
18. C. S. Lewis, "A Slip of the Tongue" in *The Weight of Glory and Other Addresses*, 141.
19. C. S. Lewis, *The Horse and His Boy* (New York: HarperCollins, 1994), 215.
20. C. S. Lewis, *The Problem of Pain*, 61.
21. C. S. Lewis, *The Last Battle* (New York: HarperCollins, 1994), 153.

PART III

THE FULLNESS OF TIME—
*THE LION, THE WITCH
AND THE WARDROBE*

will never forget my joy when Aslan invites Susan and Lucy to romp with him. For the first time I felt the elation of Christ's rising to new life.

—ANDREW CUNEO

12

The Lion, the Witch and the Wardrobe at Fifty: A Celebration (and a Worry)

Paul F. Ford

Professor Paul Ford teaches systematic theology and liturgy at St. John's Seminary, Camarillo, California. Ford is the author of *Companion to Narnia*. He contributed eleven major entries to *The C. S. Lewis Reader's Encyclopedia*, Jeffrey D. Schultz and John G. West, Jr., eds.

It is the author who intends; the book means. The author's intention is that which, if it is realized, will in his eyes constitute success. . . . The meaning of a book is the series or systems of emotions, reflections, and attitudes produced by reading it. . . . This product differs with different readers. . . . The ideally true or right meaning would be that shared . . . by the largest number of the best readers after repeated and careful readings over several generations, different periods,

> ONE OF THE JOYS OF HEAVEN WILL BE TO SIT IN THE COMPANY OF C. S. LEWIS AND ALL THE READERS OF *THE LION, THE WITCH AND THE WARDROBE* TO SHARE THE MEANING OF THIS MARVELOUS BOOK AND HOW IT ENRICHED EACH OF US.

nationalities, moods, degrees of alertness, private pre-occupations, states of health, spirits, and the like cancelling one another out when . . . they cannot be fused so as to enrich one another.[1]

That the readers of *The Lion, the Witch and the Wardrobe* now number in the millions and that their ranks will grow in the new millennium are incontestable. I suspect that one of the joys of heaven will be to sit in the company of C. S. Lewis and all the readers (and rereaders!) of *The Lion, the Witch and the Wardrobe* to share the meaning of this marvelous book and how it enriched each of us. The very sharing would be a mystagogy, a further-up-and-further-in increase of grace, grace given by the not-safe-but-good One by his death, resurrection, rescue of those turned to stone, killing of his killer, crowning of regents, and quiet slipping away to return again. What a grace! Such a sharing! This essay, far from being the appreciation[2] *The Lion, the Witch and the Wardrobe* deserves, is better read as an invitation to this celestial celebration.

Before I began this essay, it had been at least three years since I reread *The Lion,* the Witch and the Wardrobe for my contributions to *The C. S. Lewis Reader's Encyclopedia*.[3] I first read *The Lion, the Witch and the Wardrobe* thirty-three years ago when I was recovering from the flu as a junior (third-year student) in a seminary (boarding) college. For the five years previous I had been reading all of Lewis I could get my hands on. I never knew he had written children's books until I discovered them in a bookshop. Buying them rather shamefacedly (like Susan Pevensie, I wanted to appear "beyond" such childish things), I did not display them on my seminary bookshelves. However, there came the time when, sick of and in my new school, I took them out one by one and read them furtively, quickly hiding each under my bedcovers when a fellow seminarian visited me.

I will never forget my joy when— in chapter 15, "Deeper Magic from Before the Dawn of Time"—Aslan invites Susan and Lucy to romp with him. For the first time I felt the elation of Christ's rising to new life.

Of course there were other delights: the hominess of Mr. Tumnus's cave and the Beavers' lodge, the thrill of the first pronunciation of Aslan's name (the pivotal thirty-fifth and thirty-sixth full paragraphs

REMEMBER YOUR FAIRY TALES.

SPELLS ARE USED FOR BREAKING ENCHANTMENTS AS WELL AS FOR INDUCING THEM. AND YOU AND I HAVE NEED OF THE STRONGEST SPELL THAT CAN BE FOUND TO WAKE US FROM THE EVIL ENCHANTMENT OF WORLDLINESS WHICH HAS BEEN LAID UPON US FOR NEARLY A HUNDRED YEARS.

—C. S. LEWIS, "THE WEIGHT OF GLORY"

CAIR PARAVEL

of chapter 7, "A Day with the Beavers"—more about this shortly), the end of winter and the return of spring—and terrors, and revulsion (at Edmund's betrayal of Lucy). But Lewis succeeded in his goal of helping me get past the watchful dragons at the Sunday school door[4] so that I could, almost for the first time, have my own feelings about Christian realities.

I have since reread *The Lion, the Witch and the Wardrobe* at least twenty times. I *analyzed* the book and its sisters almost a dozen times for *Companion to Narnia* (I hope its readers don't think I *dissected* the books), but my best rereadings have happened when my spirits were low. Then the books served as a seven-volume magician's book that disenchanted all that should be disenchanted and reenchanted all that should be enchanted. Here I am deliberately evoking Lucy's use of Coriakin's Book in *The Voyage of the Dawn Treader* and Lewis's magnificent sermon, "The Weight of Glory": "Remember your fairy tales. Spells are used for breaking enchantments as well as for inducing them. And you and I have need of the strongest spell that can be found to wake us from the evil enchantment of worldliness which has been laid upon us for nearly a hundred years."[5]

As I have said, I hadn't read *The Lion, the Witch and the Wardrobe* for at least three years. I had tried twice and failed to read *The Magician's Nephew* as the first of The Chronicles, as the marketers of the "new" editions[6] would wish (the "worry" of the title of this essay, and I'll come to it soon). Asked to write for *The Canadian C. S. Lewis Journal* (may God reward Stephen Schofield and his wife and the editors who keep Stephen's dream alive!), I took up the "new" hardcover edition of *The Lion, the Witch and the Wardrobe* and tried to imagine what a reader might have experienced when reading the first edition that autumn of 1950 (sometime after October 16 in the British Commonwealth and after November 7 in the United States[7]). The key to reading The Chronicles is, I reminded myself, "reading with the heart," in the apt phrase of Peter Schakel.[8]

THE KEY TO READING
THE CHRONICLES
IS "READING WITH THE HEART." —PETER SCHAKEL

The most important fact I had to *forget* in this rereading is that *The Lion, the Witch and the Wardrobe* is the first of what later grew to be seven Chronicles of Narnia, a name they received from Roger Lancelyn Green only in 1952.[9] In fact, when Lewis finished the book, in the spring of 1949, no others were planned. (He soon began to write what later became *The Magician's Nephew*, which ended up being the last Chronicle he completed.[10]) I also had to forget that it had taken Lewis nearly ten years to return to and finish *The Lion, the Witch and the Wardrobe*, a book he began at the outset of World War II when girls from London were evacuated to his home outside of Oxford.

What came across strongly to me on this rereading was how the narrative tastes of the children's books of Edith Nesbit.[11] We know that Lewis loved her Bastable books (and even refers to the Bastable family in the second paragraph of chapter I of *The Magician's Nephew*) and how some motifs from her stories *The Magic City* (1911) and "The Aunt and Anabel" (in *The Magic World*, 1912) went down deep in Lewis's imagination, only to come up in *The Lion, the Witch and the Wardrobe*.[12] The omniscient author's perspective, with a touch of the avuncular (all the talk about not shutting the wardrobe door) is alive in Nesbit and in Lewis. Lewis was saying a great deal when he told Chad Walsh in the summer of 1948 that he was "completing a children's book he has begun 'in the tradition of E. Nesbit,' when he had finished *Surprised by Joy*. (*C. S. Lewis: Apostle to the Skeptics* [1949], p. 10.)"[13]

It is significant that Lewis was writing his autobiography—about the paralysis of his spiritual life caused by the death of his mother and the Great Magician's [God's] failure to answer prayer—at the same time he was writing *The Lion, the Witch and the Wardrobe*—whose central motif is the rescue of a country and a boy from the paralysis of winter and betrayal, respectively. It appears that one of the reasons that Lewis delayed finishing his autobiography is that he was swept up in the creation of the Narnian stories. These stories allowed him to deal at the feeling level with the death of his mother (in *The Magician's Nephew*) and the estrangement from his father (glimpsed in Tirian's meeting with his father Erlian in chapter 16 of *The Last Battle*[14]) and, most importantly, with the ever good but never tame lion of Narnia. The at-least-fictional resolution of Lewis's central spiritual crisis is framed by two scenes in *The Magician's Nephew*—the scene at the beginning of chapter 12, "Strawberry's Adventure" and the scene at the end of chapter 14, "The Planting of the Tree":

"MY SON, MY SON," SAID ASLAN. "I KNOW. GRIEF IS GREAT. ONLY YOU AND I IN THIS LAND KNOW THAT YET. LET US BE GOOD TO ONE ANOTHER."

(from chapter 12)

"Yes," said Digory. He had had for a second some wild idea of saying "I'll try to help you if you'll promise to help my Mother," but he realized in time that the Lion was not at all the sort of person one could try to make bargains with. But when he had said "Yes," he thought of his Mother, and he thought of the great hopes he had had, and how they were all dying away, and a lump came in his throat and tears in his eyes, and he blurted out: "But please, please—won't you—can't you give me something that will cure Mother?" Up till then he had been looking at the Lion's great feet and the huge claws on them; now, in

his despair, he looked up at its face. What he saw surprised him as much as anything in his whole life. For the tawny face was bent down near his own and (wonder of wonders) great shining tears stood in the Lion's eyes. They were such big, bright tears compared with Digory's own that for a moment he felt as if the Lion must really be sorrier about his Mother than he was himself.

"My son, my son," said Aslan. "I know. Grief is great. Only you and I in this land know that yet. Let us be good to one another."

(from chapter 14)

"And the Witch tempted you to do another thing, my son, did she not?"

"Yes, Aslan. She wanted me to take an apple home to Mother."

"Understand, then, that it would have healed her; but not to your joy or hers. The day would have come when both you and she would have looked back and said it would have been better to die in that illness."

And Digory could say nothing, for tears choked him and he gave up all hopes of saving his Mother's life; but at the same time he knew that the Lion knew what would have happened, and that there might be things more terrible even than losing someone you love by death. But now Aslan was speaking again, almost in a whisper:

"That is what would have happened, child, with a stolen apple. It is not what will happen now. What I give you now will bring joy. It will not, in your world, give endless life, but it will heal. Go. Pluck her an apple from the Tree."

Such enormous, indeed tragic, feelings were only hinted at in *The Lion, the Witch and the Wardrobe*. But all four children, especially Edmund, are quite disoriented by being evacuated from wartime London and separated from their parents. In addition Edmund has been influenced for the worst by a "horrid school which was where he had begun to go wrong."[15] (Alas, the strong, negative hint given by the kind of animal Edmund hopes to see while at the professor's estate, "snakes"—introduced into all U.S. editions by Lewis himself—has been suppressed in favor of "foxes" in all British editions[16]). However, far from hints, what are clear and unmistakable on every page, beginning with the advent of Father Christmas[17] in chapter 10, "The Spell Begins to Break," are the effects of Aslan's return, in first the sounds, then the sights, and finally the smells of spring come to Narnia. This cavalcade ends in the beholding of Aslan for the very first time—one of the most significant passages in the book.

But as for Aslan himself, the Beavers and the children didn't know what to do or say when they saw him. People who have not been in Narnia sometimes think that a thing cannot be good and terrible at the same time. If the children had ever thought so, they were cured of it now. For when they tried to look at Aslan's face they just caught a glimpse of the golden mane and the great, royal, solemn, overwhelming eyes; and then they found they couldn't look at him and went all trembly.[18]

This experience of the simultaneous terror and delight, the *mysterium tremendum et fascinans*, of Rudolf Otto's *The Idea of the Holy*, one of Lewis's ten favorite books,[19] has been anticipated in the thirty-fifth and thirty-sixth full paragraphs of chapter 7, "A Day with the Beavers":

[Mr. Beaver says, after much caution at being overheard,] "They say Aslan is on the move—perhaps has already landed."

And now a very curious thing happened. None of the children knew who Aslan was any more than you do; but the moment the Beaver had spoken these words everyone felt quite different.

. . . WHEN THEY TRIED TO LOOK AT *A*SLAN'S FACE THEY JUST CAUGHT A GLIMPSE OF THE GOLDEN MANE AND THE GREAT, ROYAL, SOLEMN EYES; AND THEN THEY FOUND THEY COULDN'T LOOK AT HIM AND THEY WENT ALL TREMBLY.

—C. S. LEWIS, *THE LION, THE WITCH AND THE WARDROBE*

Perhaps it has sometimes happened to you in a dream that someone says something which you don't understand but in the dream it feels as if it had some enormous meaning—either a terrifying one which turns the whole dream into a nightmare or else a lovely meaning too lovely to put into words, which makes the dream so beautiful that you remember it all your life and are always wishing you could get into that dream again. It was like that now.[20] At the name of Aslan each one of the children felt something jump in its inside. Edmund felt a sensation of mysterious horror. Peter felt suddenly brave and adventurous. Susan felt as if some delicious smell or some delightful strain of music had just floated by her. And Lucy got the feeling you have when you wake up in the morning and realize that it is the beginning of the holidays or the beginning of summer.

What is also obvious and splendid but so much more solemn is Edmund's reconciliation with the good and terrible Aslan and with his brother and sisters—no wonder that such an experience should have made him a grave and quiet man, great in council, King Edmund the Just.[21]

S O THEY LIVED IN GREAT JOY AND IF THEY EVER REMEMBERED THEIR LIFE IN THIS WORLD IT WAS ONLY AS ONE REMEMBERS A DREAM.

THE HUNTING OF THE WHITE STAG

After rereading I also felt how complete in itself the story was and how satisfying, if read with the heart. The book seems to come to an end in the twenty-second full paragraph of chapter 16, "The Hunting of the White Stag": "So they lived in great joy and if ever they remembered their life in this world it was only as one remembers a dream." I grew convinced that C. S. Lewis added the last two sentences in the book only when he decided to write more books in the year after he finished *The Lion, the Witch and the Wardrobe*: "And that is the very end of the adventure of the wardrobe. But if the Professor was right it was only the beginning of the adventures of Narnia." Here is where I must express my worry. Beginning with the worldwide editions published in 1994, the decision was made to market The Chronicles in the order of their internal chronology rather than in the order in which they were published from 1950–1994 (what Doris Myers call the chronological order as opposed to the canonical order). The HarperCollins Web site now announces:

> The seven books of *The Chronicles of Narnia* were published between 1950 and 1956. *The Lion, the Witch and the Wardrobe* came first—it was because of the popularity of this book that the

other books were written. But the author later expressed a wish that the books be sequenced by Narnian chronology, rather than the order in which they were first published. Thus the series now begins with *The Magician's Nephew*, in which the world of Narnia is created, and ends with *The Last Battle*, in which it is destroyed—so that a new world can begin.[22]

My worry is that this decision will diminish their impact on future readers, indeed will impede readers from moving from *The Magician's Nephew* to *The Lion, the Witch and the Wardrobe* and thus to the end. Consider how *The Lion, the Witch and the Wardrobe* introduces the mystery of a world within a wardrobe and builds to the revelation of Aslan. Contrariwise, *The Magician's Nephew* plops the reader unmysteriously into the plot of the whole series, using "Narnia" as the fortieth word a reader will now encounter.

But the pivotal insight which clinches the argument is found in the scene cited above: "None of the children knew who Aslan was *any more than you do*; but the moment the Beaver had spoken these words everyone felt quite different." The five words I have emphasized show that we must read the books in the order in which they first came

NONE OF THE CHILDREN KNEW WHO ASLAN WAS *ANY MORE THAN YOU DO*; BUT THE MOMENT THE BEAVER HAD SPOKEN THESE WORDS EVERYONE FELT QUITE DIFFERENT.

to the attention of the world of readers and rereaders, in the order in which the *meaning* of these glorious books grew beyond Lewis's late-formed *intention* to revise them.[23] Here I am referring to a sentence in epigraph of this essay: "It is the author who *intends*; the book *means*." C. S. Lewis's intention to emend the books—agreed to just two days before he died—is inferior to his attention to their meaning and their success at that level (his deeper intention). This deeper intention (I am tempted to call it the "Deeper Magic") was never better expressed than in Lewis's letter to Anne of March 5, 1961 (referring, it would seem, to her question about the twelfth from the last paragraph of chapter 16 of *The Silver Chair*):

What Aslan meant when he said he had died is, in one sense plain enough. Read the earlier book in this series called *The Lion, the Witch and the Wardrobe*, and you will find the full story of how he was killed by the White Witch and came to life again. When you have read that, I think you will probably see that there is a deeper meaning behind it. The whole Narnian story is about Christ. That is to say, I asked myself, "Supposing that there really was a world like Narnia and supposing it had (like our world) gone wrong and supposing Christ wanted to

THE WHOLE NARNIAN STORY IS ABOUT **CHRIST.**
—C. S. LEWIS

ASLAN

go into that world and save it (as He did ours) what might have happened?" The stories are my answers. Since Narnia is a world of Talking Beasts, I thought He would become a Talking Beast there, as He became a man here. I pictured Him becoming a lion there because (a) the lion is supposed to be the king of beasts; (b) Christ is called "The Lion of Judah" in the Bible; (c) I'd been having strange dreams about lions when I began writing the work. The whole series works out like this (*see list on next page*).

Here Lewis indicates that the redemption story is foundational to the meaning of the series. Even though there are inconsistencies between the stories, I shudder to think what might have happened if Lewis had applied his waning energies to making the Narnia Chronicles more successful at such a superficial level.

Most Lewis scholars I have read express the same worry. Doris Myers (in her essential essay, "Growing in Grace: The Anglican Spiritual Style in the Narnia Chronicles"[25]), Colin N. Manlove,[26] Peter Schakel,[27] and now Emma Dunbar[28] all argue to retain the original order of publication. Schakel says it most succinctly: "The only reason to read *The Magician's Nephew* first . . . is for the chronological order of events, and that, as every storyteller knows, is quite unimportant as a reason. Often the early events in a sequence have a greater impact or effect as a flashback, told after later events which provide background and establish perspective. So it is . . . with The Chronicles. The artistry, the archetypes, and the pattern of Christian thought all make it preferable to read the books in the order of their publication."[29]

We will have to see how the new marketing strategy will work out. We can pray that if sales of the Chronicles diminish, a return to the canonical order will be ordered.

And, after all, the strategy is not consistent. Isn't it amazing that, whenever anything Narnian is marketed, it is *The Lion, the Witch and the Wardrobe* that is featured! Witness the Michael Hague wall calendars,[30] the seven special editions Hooper mentions in his *C. S. Lewis: A Companion and Guide*,[31] a list which includes the glorious fully illustrated Robin Laurie abridgement (how I wish he would finish the other six Chronicles!), and the nine of the eleven projects since Hooper's book was published in 1996: (1) *Lucy Steps through the Wardrobe*, (2) *Edmund and the White Witch*, (3) *Aslan*,

(4) *Aslan's Triumph*, (5) *The 1999 World of Narnia Calendar*, (6) *The Narnia Paper Dolls: The Lion, the Witch and the Wardrobe Collection* [these six books are illustrated by Deborah Maze], (7) *The Lion, the Witch and the Wardrobe: A 2001 Calendar*, (8) *The Lion, the Witch and the Wardrobe* (with illustrations by Christian Birmingham), (9) *The Lion, the Witch and the Wardrobe* (pictures in black and white and full color by Pauline Baynes). Only in 1999 do we see (10) *A Book of Narnians: The Lion, the Witch and the Others* (as well as a second edition of *The Land of Narnia: Brian Sibley Explores the World of C. S. Lewis*, originally published in 1989). And only in the year 2000 do we see an adapted and illustrated edition of a section of (11) *The Magician's Nephew: The Wood between the Worlds*. But even the HarperCollins Classroom Activity Guide to The Chronicles of Narnia shows *The Lion, the Witch and the Wardrobe* as first on page two of the PDF file at their Web site.

So, happy birthday to *The Lion, the Witch and the Wardrobe*. May it find new readers for centuries to come so that readers will thrill at and know the name and the deeds of the Son of the emperor-beyond-the-seas.

ENDNOTES:

1. C. S. Lewis, "On Criticism," *Of Other Worlds: Essays and Stories*, Walter Hooper, ed. (New York: Harcourt, Brace & World, 1966), 57 (Lewis's emphasis).

2. The dictionaries tell us that to *appreciate* is "to make or form an estimate of worth, quality, or amount, to perceive the full force of, or to esteem adequately or highly, to recognize as valuable or excellent, or to find worth in."

3. Jeffrey D. Schultz and John G. West, eds. (Grand Rapids, Mich.: Zondervan, 1998): Arthur James Balfour; *Books of Influence:* Chronicles of Narnia: *The Horse and His Boy; The Last Battle; The Lion, the Witch and the Wardrobe;* George MacDonald; *The Magician's Nephew; Prince Caspian; The Silver Chair; The Voyage of the Dawn Treader*, q.v.

4. C. S. Lewis, "Sometimes Fairy Stories May Say Best What's to Be Said," *Of Other Worlds: Essays and Stories*, 37.

5. There are so many editions that I refer you to the fifth full paragraph.

6. The 1994 HarperCollins world trade hard- and soft-cover editions and the mass-market paperback edition.

7. Walter Hooper, *C. S. Lewis: A Companion and Guide* (New York: HarperCollins, 1996), 452, 454. Hooper makes available a few of the first British reviews on 449–450.

8. Peter Shakel, *Reading with the Heart: The Way into Narnia* (Grand Rapids, Mich.: William B. Eerdmans, 1979).

9. Roger Lancelyn Green and Walter Hooper, *C. S. Lewis: A Biography* (London: Collins, 1974), 245.

10. See my entry, "Chronicles of Narnia," in *The C. S. Lewis Reader's Encyclopedia*, Schultz and West, eds. (Grand Rapids: Zondervan, 1998).

11. Edith Nesbit (1858–1924). In the *Oxford Companion to English Literature* (1985) Margaret Drabble tells us that "she is remembered . . . for her children's books, tales of everyday family life sometimes mingled with magic. In 1898 her first stories about the young Bastables appeared with such success that she published three 'Bastable' novels in quick succession: *The Story of the Treasure-Seekers* (1899), *The Wouldbegoods* (1901), and *The New Treasure-Seekers* (1904). Other well-known titles with a lasting appeal include *Five Children and It* (1902), *The Phoenix and the Carpet* (1904), *The Railway Children* (1906), and *The Enchanted Castle* (1907)."

12. It is significant that the child heroes of *The Magic City* and "The Aunt and Anabel" have their respective experiences in imaginary worlds in order to help them repair relationships they have damaged, Philip Haldane with his stepsister Lucy and Anabel (no last name given) with her great aunt.

13. Green and Hooper, *C. S. Lewis: A Biography*, 238.

14. Who can miss seeing the long evenings of a Northern Ireland summer in the following (p. 204 in the 1994 hardcover and trade paperback editions)?

    But before [Tirian] had had much time to think of this he felt two strong arms thrown about him and felt a bearded kiss on his cheeks and heard a well remembered voice saying:

    "What, lad? Art thicker and taller since I last touched thee!"

    It was his own father, the good King Erlian: but not as Tirian had seen him last when they brought him home pale and wounded from his fight with the giant, nor even as Tirian remembered him in his later years when he was a grayheaded warrior. This was his father, young and merry, as he could just remember him from very early days when he himself had been a little boy playing games with his father in the castle garden at Cair Paravel, just before bedtime on summer evenings. The very smell of the bread-and-milk he used to have for supper came back to him.

15. Chapter 16, "The Hunting of the White Stag," ninth full paragraph. For a more extensive discussion of Edmund's character and development, please see "Edmund Pevensie" in *Companion to Narnia*.

16. Edmund's excitement over "snakes" and Susan's excitement over "rabbits" in the British version for "foxes" in the American foreshadow Edmund's fall into evil and Susan's fall into vanity. Due to trade and union regulations at the time, all The Chronicles of Narnia were typeset first in England and then all over again in the U.S.; Lewis had to correct two different sets of galleys and made changes at that time. See "Variants" in "Using the Companion" in all but the first edition of *Companion to Narnia*.

17. A typographical error persists from the very first editions to the latest. When Mr. Beaver calls his wife and the children from the hiding place to see Father Christmas, he says, "Come out, Sons and Daughters of Adam," when there is only one Son of Adam, Peter, there.

18. Chapter 12, "Peter's First Battle," eighth full paragraph.

19. Rudolf Otto, *The Idea of the Holy: An Inquiry into the Non-rational Factor in the Idea of the Divine and Its Relation to the Rational*, John W. Harvey, tr. (Oxford:

Oxford, 1923). Lewis identified it as one of his "top ten" in *The Christian Century* 79:23 (June 6, 1962), 719.

20. How much this simile is like the one in the all U.S. editions of what used to be in the eleventh full paragraph from chapter 12, "The Dark Island," of *The Voyage of the Dawn Treader*, now disappeared from all further editions: "And just as there are moments when simply to lie in bed and see the daylight pouring through your window and to hear the cheerful voice of an early postman or milkman down below and to realize that *it was only a dream: it wasn't real*, is so heavenly that it was very nearly worth having the nightmare in order to have the joy of waking; so they all felt when they came out of the dark."

21. The summary statement found in chapter 16, "The Hunting of the White Stag," twenty-first full paragraph.

22. *The HarperCollins Classroom Activity Guide to The Chronicles of Narnia*, page three of the PDF file at www.narnia.com.

23. "His last visitor was Kaye Webb, editor of Puffin Books in which *The Chronicles of Narnia* were appearing. 'We had a nice talk on Wednesday,' she wrote to Green, who had arranged the meeting. 'What a very great and dear man. How I wish I'd had a chance to know him well, but how grateful I am that you "introduced" us to each other. He promised to re-edit the books (connect the things that didn't tie up) and he asked me to come again,'" Green and Hooper, *C. S. Lewis*, 307.

24. Hooper, *C. S. Lewis: A Companion and Guide*, 426.

25. The last edition is in David Mills, *C. S. Lewis and the Art of Witness* (Grand Rapids, Mich.: William B. Eerdmans, 1998), 185–202.

26. Colin N. Manlove, *C. S. Lewis: His Literary Achievement* (New York: St. Martin's Press, 1987), 124–25 and *The Chronicles of Narnia: The Patterning of a Fantastic World* (New York: Twayne Publishers [Twayne Masterwork Studies No. 127], 1993), 111–15.

27. Peter Schakel, *Reading with the Heart: The Way into Narnia* (Grand Rapids: William B. Eerdmans Publishing Co., 1979) and "Elusive Birds and Narrative Nets: The Appeal of Story in C. S. Lewis's Chronicles of Narnia" in Andrew Walker and James Patrick, eds., *A Christian for All Christians: Essays in Honor of C. S. Lewis* (New York: Regnery Gateway, 1992), 116–31.

28. Dunbar is the granddaughter of Maureen Moore, Lady Dunbar of Hempbriggs. She wrote her 1998 senior dissertation at Scotland's St. Andrew's University on the subject; its title is "The Wardrobe or the Rings? What is the best way to read C. S. Lewis's The Chronicles of Narnia: canonical or chronological."

29. Schakel, *Reading with the Heart*, 143.

30. For 1982; this calendar and the one for 1983 on Prince Caspian was intended to be a seven-year project of the Lewis estate and the Episcopal Radio-TV Foundation.

31. Hooper, *C. S. Lewis*, 454.

Lewis seemed instinctively to relish mixing religious and mythical elements together.

FATHER CHRISTMAS GIVES GIFTS
TO LUCY, PETER, & SUSAN

13

"DEEPER MAGIC":
ALLUSIONS IN *THE LION, THE WITCH AND THE WARDROBE*

MARVIN D. HINTEN

Marvin D. "Marv" Hinten, an English professor at Friends University in Wichita, Kansas, did his doctoral dissertation on The Chronicles of Narnia; his most recent book is *The Keys to the Chronicles*, published by Broadman & Holman. Parts of this piece were first published in the C. S. Lewis journal *The Lamp-Post*. It also appears as part of a just-published book by Broadman & Holman covering allusions in the entire Narnian series.

The most clearly biblical of the seven Chronicles of Narnia, *The Lion, the Witch and the Wardrobe* (hereafter *Lion*) incorporates numerous elements of the suffering, death, and resurrection of Christ. Lewis didn't originally intend to rewrite the life of Christ as a children's fairy tale, as he once noted in an article on fairy tales:

Some people seem to think that I began by asking myself how I could say something about Christianity to children; then fixed on the fairy tale as an instrument; then collected information about child psychology and decided what age-group I'd write for; then drew up a list of basic Christian truths and hammered out "allegories" to embody them. This is all pure moonshine. I couldn't write in that way at all. Everything began with images; a faun carrying an umbrella, a queen on a sledge, a magnificent lion. At first there wasn't even anything Christian about them; that element pushed itself in of its own accord.[1]

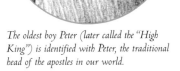

The oldest boy Peter (later called the "High King") is identified with Peter, the traditional head of the apostles in our world.

When Lewis first attempted to form these images into a story in 1939, there doesn't appear to be anything biblical about them: "This book is about four children whose names were Ann, Martin, Rose, and Peter. But it is most about Peter who was the youngest."[2] Two significant changes differentiate this from the actual opening, which Lewis wrote in the late 1940s: "Once there were four children whose names were Peter, Susan, Edmund and Lucy."[3] In the original attempt Ann would have presumably been the oldest, which generally carries some leadership responsibilities; the alteration puts Peter in the headship role, which Lewis always felt belonged to a male. In addition, since the children to a considerable degree play the role of Aslan's "disciples" in the book, the name change identifies Peter (later the "High King") with Peter, the traditional head of the apostles in our world.

Jesus' three disciples, Peter, James, and John, formed a sort of inner circle, being present at situations such as the transfiguration and the garden of Gethsemane prayer that the other apostles missed. Peter, Susan, and Lucy prove analogues to these three. (Since Lewis did not originally plan a sequel, he did not know at this time that Susan would later leave the "disciples.") If Peter parallels the apostle Peter, then Lucy parallels John, the disciple "whom Jesus loved," as he is repeatedly described in the book of John (20:2; 21:7, etc.). Throughout the series Lucy represents the one most dedicated to goodness and the one to whom Aslan appears most frequently and displays the most tenderness. Owen Barfield's daughter, to whom Lewis as "affectionate Godfather" dedicated the book, probably provided her name. Owen Barfield was Lewis's lifelong attorney and friend.

The idea to have the four children leave London and stay with a single professor during

Throughout the series Lucy represents the one most dedicated to goodness and the one to whom Aslan appears most frequently and displays the most tenderness.

the war lay rooted in reality. Lewis and his household kept several children from London "because of the air-raids," as the novel says. The adventures start because a "steady rain falling" forces the children to explore the house, "the sort of house that you never seem to come to the end of."[4] In his autobiography, Lewis says, "I am a product of long corridors [and] . . . attics explored in solitude," which he examined during "endless rainy afternoons."[5]

Upon entering the land of Narnia, arguably named after an "ancient Italian city"[6] according to Lewis's secretary Walter Hooper, Lucy meets the faun Mr. Tumnus, whose name seems an abbreviated form of Vertumnus, the Roman god of the seasons and of growth. Through the power of Vertumnus the seasons changed and growth took place. Yet in Narnia the faun Tumnus obviously retains no power, and Narnia remains a land (at least when we meet Tumnus) where the seasons never change and nothing ever grows.

Mr. Tumnus, the faun who befriends Lucy, may have been named after Vertumnus, the Roman god of the seasons and of growth.

When Lucy tells Tumnus she has entered Narnia through the wardrobe in the spare room, he refers to her as the girl from "the far land of Spare Oom where eternal summer reigns around the bright city of War Drobe."[7] Brian Sibley suggests as an inspiration for this Edith Nesbit's "The Aunt and Anabel," where the magic land is reached via "Bigwardrobeinspareroom."[8]

When Peter and Susan hear Lucy's unbelievable tale of Narnia, they take their concern to the professor with whom they are staying. Though *Lion* doesn't reveal his name (presumably Lewis had not determined it yet), we learn in *The Magician's Nephew* that this is Digory Kirke, a surname filled with meaning for Lewis. "Kirk" is Old Norse (as well as Scottish) for church; thus, at least indirectly, the children find their way to Aslan's country through the church. In fact, Lewis had already used "kirk" for church in his 1930s allegory, *The Pilgrim's Regress*. Edmund Spenser's use of the word in *The Faerie Queene* may have nudged Lewis toward it as well. And on a different but equally applicable level, "Kirk" is short for Kirkpatrick, the retired professor who served as a tutor

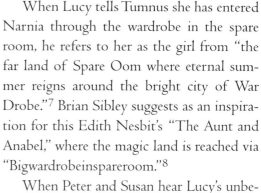

during Lewis's teenage years and for whom he always retained the utmost respect. With one word Lewis hereby invests the story with linguistic, literary, and biographical layers.

During Peter and Susan's conversations with Professor Kirke occurs the first example of "autography" —Lewis's borrowing of phrases or concepts from his adult theological nonfiction for his children's fiction. Professor Kirke asks the children to think about Lucy and her improbable story logically: "There are only three possibilities. Either your sister is telling lies, or she is mad, or she is telling the truth. You know she doesn't tell lies and it is obvious that she is not mad. For the moment then and unless any further evidence turns up, we must assume that she is telling the truth."9

It would be difficult for anyone familiar with *Mere Christianity* to read this and not be reminded of Lewis's famous "liar, lunatic, or Lord" trilemma: "A man who was merely a man and said the sort of things Jesus said would not be a great moral teacher. He would either be a lunatic—on a level with the man who says he is a poached egg— or else he would be the Devil of Hell.

"Kirk" is short for Kirkpatrick, the retired professor who served as a tutor during Lewis's teenage years and for whom he always retained the utmost respect.

You must make your choice. Either this man was, and is, the Son of God: or else a madman or something worse."10

Lewis claimed not to have begun with theology in mind, but approximately one-fourth of the way into the novel, theology certainly influenced his thinking (at least in revision) early on.

When the four children finally enter Narnia together, they see a sign proclaiming the wrath of Queen Jadis, the white witch, signed by her wolf police captain, Fenris Ulf. (British editions name him "Maugrim," with obvious connotations of "grim maw," or fierce mouth). "Jadis" means "of old" in French, as in Francois Villon's medieval lyric, "Ballade des Dames de Temps Jadis" ("Ballad of the Women of Yesteryear"). The word certainly fits a being who has been alive for well over a thousand years.

Queen Jadis, the white witch, comes from the word "jadis": "of old," which is fitting because she has been alive for well over a thousand years. Her wolf police captain, Maugrim, connotes the term "grim maw," or fierce mouth.

129

"Jadis" also contains connotations of "false jade," a phrase used elsewhere in The Chronicles by Lewis[11] as a term of abuse (from Renaissance usage). Under the witch's spell Narnia becomes a land of unending winter, corresponding to the dreaded perpetual winter, or *fimbulvetr*, of Norse myth.[12] For ancient Scandinavian people the worst plight imaginable would be to live in a land where spring thaw never came. That fear was woven into their mythology, and Lewis pictures the myth here.

As for the witch's captain, "ulf" is Old Norse for wolf, and Fenris is clearly a form of Fenrir, the wolf-son of evil god Loki in Norse mythology, who bit off the hand of Tyr, god of victory. Traditionally a symbol of fierceness and destruction, Fenrir destroys Odin, chief of all the Norse gods, at Ragnarok, the ending of the world in Norse myth. Fenris's close association with the witch parallels Fenrir's strong relationship with Loki, the evil Norse god.

The children hear from Mr. Beaver about Aslan, the Christ figure of The Chronicles. Fittingly, a lion represents Aslan. Tradition labels the lion the "King of beasts" (as Mr. Beaver

Tradition labels the lion the "king of the beasts"; Aslan is further proclaimed "King of the beasts."

proclaims Aslan, with a capital "K," in the eighth chapter). One of the biblical names for Christ, "Lion of the tribe of Judah" appears in Revelation 5:5 (KJV), where under that name Christ demonstrates his power by opening seven unbroken seals. *Aslan*, the Turkish word for lion, Lewis gleaned from Edward Lane's translation of *Arabian Nights*, according to a 1952 letter.[13]

Why was Lewis reading translations of *Arabian Nights* shortly before writing *Lion*? In the late 1940s he had a Middle Eastern pupil, M. A. Manzalaoui, who eventually did his Oxford thesis on the subject of pre-twentieth-century English translations of Arabic works. Edward Lane, a nineteenth-century English writer, did one of the main Victorian-era translations of *Arabian Nights*. Given Lewis's conscientious efforts as a thesis director, I imagine he reread Lane's translation while working with Manzalaoui as a student, and thus the word *Aslan* had been on his mind a good bit as he prepared to begin The Chronicles.

The Turkish derivation of the word *Aslan* appears to be perhaps the only exception in The Chronicles to the rule that anything Arabic or Turkish-sounding

or favoring Turkish ways proves bad. (It will be remembered that the witch had won Edmund to her side with Turkish delight.) Medieval Christians (and thus Lewis) remembered the Arabs as the feared villains from the south who nearly conquered Europe in the eighth century and the Turks as the infidels who had taken the holy city of Jerusalem and spilled so much Christian blood during the Crusades.

After Mr. Beaver quotes one of the "old rhymes" (the Narnian equivalent of prophecy), he tells the children about the witch, descended on one side from giants and on the other side from the jinn. In Norse mythology the giants perpetually undermined the work of the gods. The jinn, supernatural creatures of Arabic legend, exercised the power to take on human and animal shapes. Lewis grew up with Norse mythology and spent much of the late 1940s rereading Arabian myth.

Mr. Beaver tells the children four thrones await human rulers at Cair Paravel, the seacoast city that should serve as Narnia's capital. The city's name may stem from a rhythmic extension of "caravel." Caravels were the sailing vessels that began to be used in Europe in the fifteenth century; two of Columbus's three ships, including his flagship, were caravels.[14] An Old Norse word, Middle English translated *cair* as meaning "to go."

The name of "Cair Paravel," the sea coast city that should serve as Narnia's capital, may stem from a rhythmic extension of "caravel."

C. S. Lewis as a young boy, photographed with a favorite toy.

Occasionally, it helped form Norse place names; thus J. R. R. Tolkien uses it as part of the name of Cair Andros, an island in *The Return of the King*.[15]

The Beavers and the children flee from the witch across the countryside and meet Father Christmas. This figure particularly drew Tolkien's ire as an intrusion of legend into a section of the story related to the coming of Christ into the world. Brian Sibley's *The Land of Narnia* contains a picture of Lewis as a child beside what Sibley labels one of his favorite toys— Father Christmas riding on a donkey. That toy blended in itself two elements of Christmas; for the donkey, in combination with the season, suggests the one Mary rode on her trip from Galilee to Bethlehem. Even as a preschooler Lewis seemed instinctively to relish mixing religious and mythical elements together.

THE GIFTS:

Peter is given a shield and a sword. In the famous "whole armor of God" passage in Ephesians 6, the shield embodies faith, and the sword represents the Word of God. Susan obtains a horn that can bring help, analogous to prayer, and Lucy receives a cordial with supernatural restorative powers, representing the gift of healing.

Father Christmas distributes gifts to the children, which somewhat parallel the spiritual gifts given to the church in another such blending. Peter is given a shield and a sword. In the famous "whole armor of God" passage in Ephesians 6, the shield embodies faith, and the sword represents the Word of God. Susan obtains a horn that can bring help, analogous to prayer, and Lucy receives a cordial with supernatural restorative powers, representing the gift of healing. (Susan also gains a bow and arrows; if this has a spiritual parallel, I am unable to determine it. But with Lewis, unlike Tolkien and most other writers, blending allusive and nonallusive elements proved his most common technique.)

As Father Christmas stands allied with Aslan, the gifts also have a Norse flavor. The most common poetic name for *king* in Anglo-Saxon and Old Norse poetry is "ring-giver" (sometimes "gift-giver"). Aslan, the lord of Narnia, distributes gifts to his followers through Father Christmas, similar to what occurred in Norse myth: "Like any earthly ruler, Odin [the chief Norse god] handed out weapons to his chosen followers, and once they had received them, they were bound to give him loyal service till death and beyond it."[16] This is characteristically Lewisian: a moving back and forth from the spiritual (Aslan) to the secular (Father Christmas) to the secular with spiritual overtones (the gifts).

The children and the Beavers arrive at the stone table that lies, significantly, on a hilltop. Here Aslan will sacrifice all, just as Christian tradition has for centuries placed Calvary (where Christ was crucified) on a hill. Lewis asserted in a 1960 letter, that the stone table represented Moses' table[17]—for *table* became another word for the stone tablets upon which the Ten Commandments were inscribed, as described in Exodus 32:16: "And the tables were the work of God, and the writing was the writing of God, graven upon the tables" (KJV). (Lewis knew the King James Version of the Bible above all others, so all biblical references are to that text.) This explains both the age and the carved writing of the stone table and provides an additional reason for the hilltop location: Moses received the Ten Commandments on the top of Mt. Sinai. The pavilion (tent) "hard by" the stone table reminds us of the tabernacle, the tent of God's presence for the Old Testament Jews.

AND THE TABLES WERE THE WORK OF GOD, AND THE WRITING WAS THE WRITING OF GOD, GRAVEN UPON THE TABLES.—Exodus 32:16 (KJV)

Moses carrying the two tablets that contained the Ten Commandments.

Aslan's creatures by the stone table include an assorted mix of humans, animals, and mythological creatures; among these last are four centaurs and "a bull with the head of a man."[18] Throughout The Chronicles, creatures with an animal body and human head prove good; creatures with a human body and animal head embody bad. This symbolically represents the standard Renaissance concept of reason over passion—that in the great chain of being reason should always be elevated over passion and control it. Some of the witch's creatures are minotaurs, with human bodies and bull heads, symbolizing their perverse commitment to passion over reason; thus they join the side of evil.[19]

When the witch confronts Aslan, she reminds him of the "Deep Magic," that "every traitor belongs to me as my lawful prey and that for every treachery I have a right to a kill."[20] This seems an oblique reference to Romans 6:23, "The wages of sin is death." The word *lawful* is appropriately chosen, as the magic is written on the stone table, which represents the requirements of the Old Testament law. It is also written (in the American editions before 1994) on "the World Ash Tree," another blending of Norse and Christian elements. While the

THROUGHOUT THE CHRONICLES, CREATURES WITH AN ANIMAL BODY AND HUMAN HEAD PROVE GOOD; CREATURES WITH A HUMAN BODY AND ANIMAL HEAD EMBODY BAD.

CENTAUR

MINOTAUR

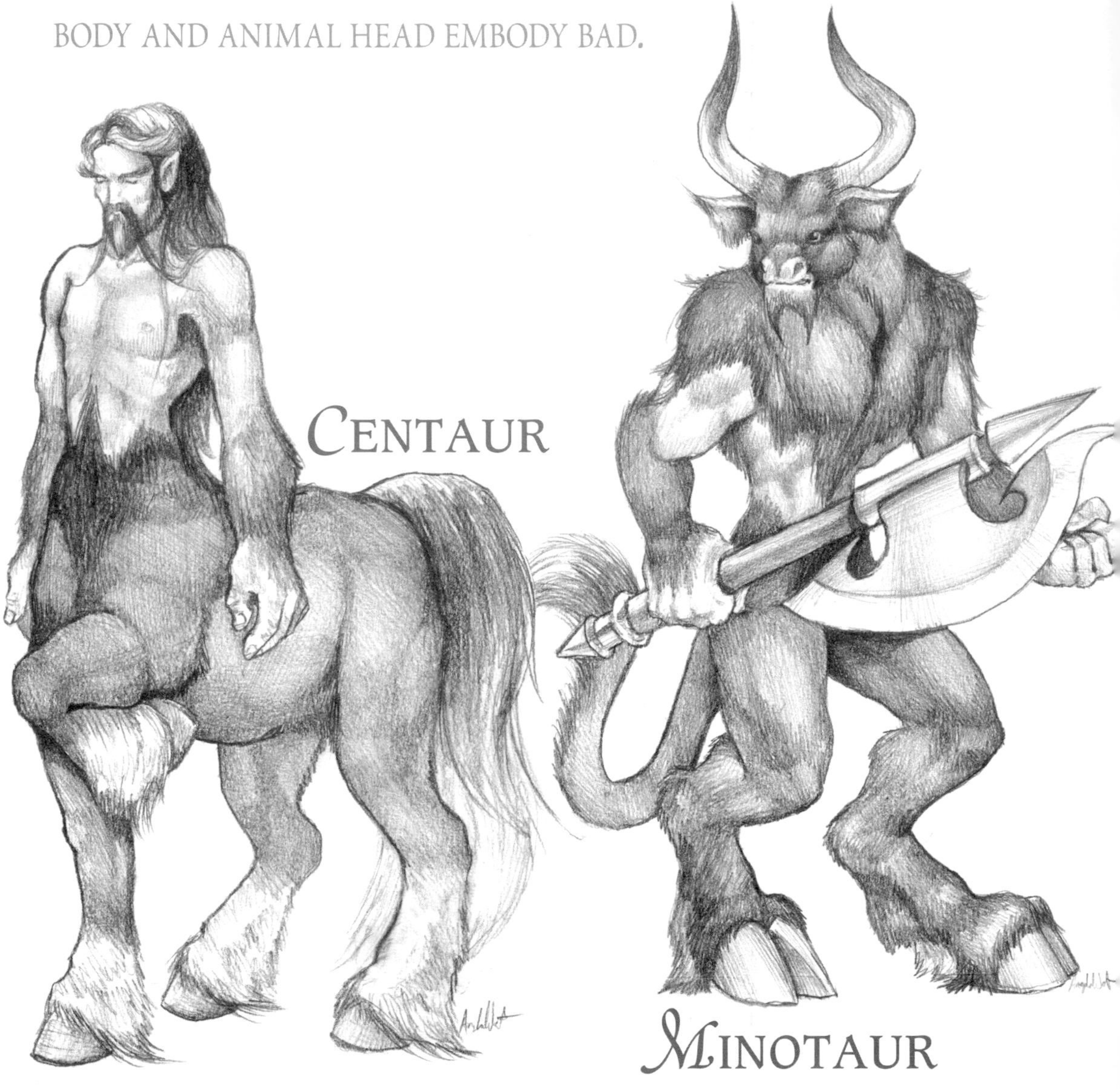

stone table (which according to the white witch has been used for sacrifice before) represents a symbol of death, the Norse regarded the World Ash Tree, or Yggdrasill, as a symbol of life. Dew from this tree provided nourishment for two humans while the rest of the world was undergoing the long winter.[21] Symbolically, then, the Old Testament law provided nourishment during the time before the sacrifice of Christ.

The witch tells Aslan that because of Edmund's treachery the law of Narnia requires that she be given blood, a fairly clear reference to (among other passages) Hebrews 9:22: "And almost all things are by the law purged with blood; and without shedding of blood is no remission [forgiveness]"(KJV). Without this act, Narnia will be destroyed with fire and water, which immediately reminds biblically literate readers of Noah's flood and the prophesied final destruction of the earth by fire.

The most biblically allusive chapter of The Chronicles can be found in the fourteenth chapter of Lion, "Aslan's Passion." The similarities in this portion primarily need recognition rather than comment:

At last Peter said, "But you will be there yourself, Aslan." "I can give you no promise of that," answered the Lion.[22]

Simon Peter said unto him, "Lord, whither goest thou?" Jesus answered him, "Whither I go, thou canst not follow me now" (John 13:36 KJV).

[Aslan speaking] "I am sad and lonely. Lay your hands on my mane so that I can feel you are there and let us walk like that."[23]

Then saith he [Jesus] unto them, "My soul is exceeding sorrowful, even unto death: tarry ye here, and watch with me" (Matt. 26:38).

Had the Lion chosen, one of those paws could have been the death of them all.[24]

"Thinkest thou that I cannot now pray to my Father, and he shall presently give me more than twelve legions of angels?" (Matt. 26:53).

But he made no noise.[25]
But Jesus held his peace (Matt. 26:63).

Thickly was he surrounded by the whole crowd of creatures kicking him, hitting him, spitting on him, jeering at him.[26]

Then did they spit in his face, and buffeted him (Matt. 26:67). And the men that held Jesus mocked him, and smote [hit] him (Luke 22:63).

THE SACRIFICE OF ASLAN

"The wages of sin is death." The magic is written on the stone table, which represents the requirements of the Old Testament law.

At the end of the chapter, Aslan dies. In the middle of the night, Susan and Lucy try to untie him but aren't able to loose his cords. This parallels Mark 16:3, when the women on their way to the tomb recognize their inability to move the stone. (In the novel and the Bible, both groups caring about the body are entirely female.) But mice come along that are able to gnaw away the ropes, thus solving the plot problem and bringing in Aesop's fable at the same time. The girls notice that as dawn nears, the stars are "getting fainter—all except one very big one low down on the Eastern horizon."[27] In our world this would be Venus, or the morning star; and its presence as Aslan nears resurrection alludes to Christ's referral to himself in Revelation 22:16 as "the bright and morning star" (KJV).

Aslan's resurrection occurs just as "up came the edge of the sun."[28] Thus the Son (of the emperor-over-the-sea) rises as the sun rises. The pun on "sun" and "Son" is a frequent one in seventeenth-century religious poetry. Henry Vaughan calls his poem on attending church "Son-days"; George Herbert, in "The Son," says, "How neatly do we give one only name/To parent's issue and the sun's bright star!"[29]

At Aslan's resurrection the stone table cracks, symbolizing the end of the law and paralleling the tearing in two of the temple veil as well (Matt. 27:51). Just as the apostles in Luke 24:37 "supposed that they had seen a spirit" (KJV), Susan wonders whether Aslan is a ghost. His subsequent rescue of the statues corresponds to the traditional Harrowing of Hell, when (in medieval and Renaissance theology) Jesus rescued the souls of the Jewish patriarchs who had died before him.

Near the end of the book, when the

At Aslan's resurrection the stone table cracks, symbolizing the end of the law and paralleling the tearing in two of the temple veil as well (Matt. 27:51).

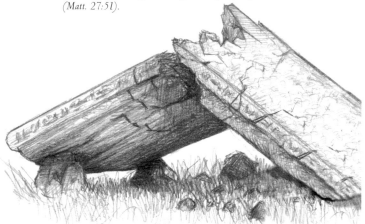

final battle is over, Lucy's cordial heals his wounds and restores him both physically and emotionally/spiritually, possibly in an allusion to James 5:15: "And the prayer of faith shall save the sick, and the Lord shall raise him up; and if he have committed sins, they shall be forgiven him" (KJV). Lucy notes that Edmund looks the best he has been "since his first term at that horrid school which was where he had begun to go wrong."[30] Although the series is written by an Oxford don (or perhaps because of that fact), schools are not treated favorably in The Chronicles. As any reader of the autobiographical *Surprised by Joy* will recall, Lewis loathed his school days. A man in his fifties who devotes 40 percent of his autobiography to telling how much he hated school has obviously been scarred for life, particularly when he entitles the first chapter on the subject "Concentration Camp."

Allusively, *Lion* is the most biblical and most Norse of The Chronicles. This interesting feature reveals a characteristic of Lewis that has been overlooked. While the charges are accurate that he mixes together images from a variety of sources, Lewis generally selects a preponderance of images that will in some way match the setting and/or theme of the book. For a warm, wet climate (as in *Caspian*), Lewis uses a large number of Greek elements; for a warm, dry climate (as in *Horse*), he uses many Arabian/Turkish elements. In the case of *Lion*, much of the Narnian portion of the book is set in the witch's eternal winter. To fit that climate Lewis uses a larger-than-usual number of Norse elements. Lewis does mix together a variety of the elements in each book, but the majority of the elements support the setting. Lewis's first Narnian novel thus richly reveals his deep knowledge of biblical and literary sources.

EDITOR'S NOTE: If you found this article informative and appealing, you'll be interested to know that my book *The Keys to the Chronicles* has just been published by Broadman & Holman. It does for all seven books in the series what this article does for *Lion*, plus it adds lots of extra information about Lewis's life and reading that I hope you'll find of great interest!

ENDNOTES:

1. C. S. Lewis, *On Stories,* Walter Hooper, ed. (New York: Harcourt Brace, 1982), 46.
2. C. S. Lewis, *The Lion, the Witch and the Wardrobe* (New York: Macmillan, 1950), 1.
3. Walter Hooper, *Past Watchful Dragons* (New York: Macmillan, 1979), 29–30.
4. Lewis, *The Lion, the Witch and the Wardrobe*, 4.
5. C. S. Lewis, *Surprised by Joy* (New York: Harcourt Brace, 1954), 10.
6. Hooper, *Past Watchful Dragons*, 108.
7. Lewis, *The Lion, the Witch and the Wardrobe*, 11.
8. Brian Sibley, *The Land of Narnia* (New York: HarperCollins, 1990), 21.
9. Lewis, *The Lion, the Witch and the Wardrobe*, 45.
10. C. S. Lewis, *Mere Christianity* (New York: Macmillan, 1952), 56.

11. C. S. Lewis, *The Horse and His Boy* (New York: Macmillan, 1954), 105.
12. H. R. Ellis Davidson, *Gods and Myths of Northern Europe* (New York: Penguin, 1964), 202.
13. C. S. Lewis, *Letters to Children*, Lyle W. Dorsett and Marjorie Lamp Mead, eds. (New York: Macmillan, 1985), 29.
14. E. R. Chamberlain, *Everyday Life in Renaissance Times* (New York: G. P. Putnam's Sons, 1965), 29.
15. J. R. R. Tolkien, *The Return of the King* (New York: Ballantine, 1965), 103.
16. Davidson, *Gods and Myths of Northern Europe*, 49.
17. Lewis, *Letters to Children*, 93.
18. Lewis, *The Lion, the Witch and the Wardrobe*, 122.
19. Ibid., 132.
20. Ibid., 139.

21. Davidson, *Gods and Myths of Northern Europe*, 202.
22. Lewis, *The Lion, the Witch and the Wardrobe*, 143.
23. Ibid., 147.
24. Ibid., 149.
25. Ibid., 150.
26. Ibid., 151.
27. Ibid., 156–57.
28. Ibid., 158.
29. Mario A. DiCesare, ed., *George Herbert and the Seventeenth-Century Religious Poets* (New York: Norton, 1978), 60, 157.
30. Lewis, *The Lion, the Witch and the Wardrobe*, 177.

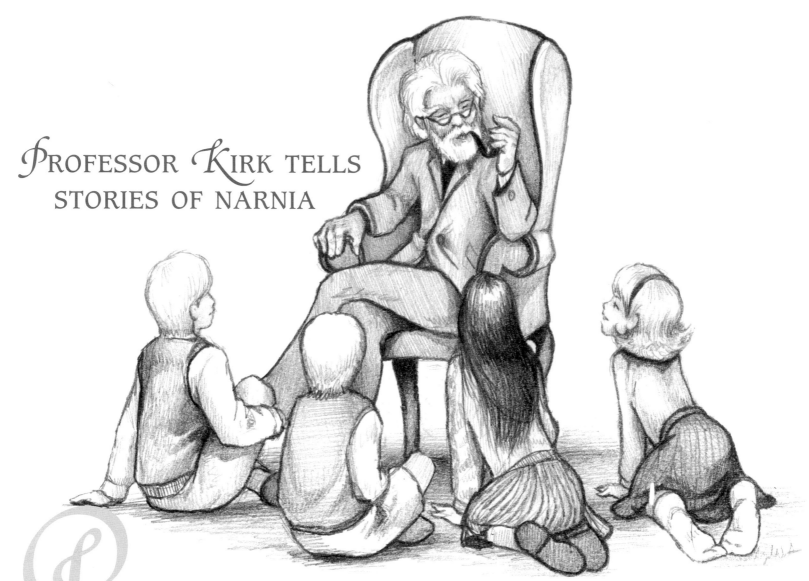

PROFESSOR KIRK TELLS
STORIES OF NARNIA

*P*rofessor Kirk (who is the same person as Digory, the boy who was present at the creation of
Narnia) knocks down the children's a priori assumptions about the nature of reality.

14

THE FASCINATION WITH "OTHER WORLDS" IN *THE LION, THE WITCH AND THE WARDROBE*

PETER KREEFT

Peter Kreeft, professor of philosophy at Boston College, has published forty-five books, including C. S. Lewis for the Third Millennium, The Shadowlands of C. S. Lewis, *and* C. S. Lewis in Christian Perspective. *Forthcoming books include* The Philosophy of Tolkien *and a novel of spiritual warfare,* An Ocean Full of Angels.

*B*efore a work of art can do anything else with us, it has to get our attention. Before a movie or a book can please, inform, challenge, satisfy, educate, edify, or relax us, it must fascinate us enough to persuade us to give it some of our time, that is, our life, our lifetime.

The three most fascinating things in *The Lion, the Witch and the Wardrobe* are, of course, the lion, the witch, and the wardrobe.

(1) THE LION

The lion certainly comes first. In creating the character of Aslan, Lewis did what no one had ever done before and what his friend Dorothy Sayers declared simply impossible: to present Jesus Christ as a credible and interesting fictional character. (Perhaps, the only other writer who did that was Dostoyevski in "The Grand Inquisitor," in which Christ utters not a single word and performs only one act.) As soon as the craftsman puts words into the mouth of The Word, the craft fails, and becomes either hokey, preachy, familiar, and boring, or else cute, clever, creative, and oh-so-original. In both cases he is obviously made in our image, for he is neither of those two things. (G. B. Shaw joked that "God created us in his image, and we have been returning him the compliment ever since.")

How did Lewis succeed? By creeping past what Walter Hooper called the two "watchful dragons" of duty and familiarity, which inhibit our heart's spontaneous response of fascination. No one in the Gospels who ever met him was bored—not his friends, not his enemies, not those who couldn't figure out whether to be his friends or his enemies. The word repeatedly used for the reaction of all three groups is *thaumadzein*, "wonder," "amazement," "fascination." *All* familiar categories failed to contain him. He took everyone off their guard.

How does Lewis let Aslan do the same to us? By a double distancing: from human to lion and from earth to Narnia. Aslan is indeed Christ, but Narnia is not Earth and The Chronicles are not an allegory of the Gospels. They are a "what if" experiment in thought and imagination: What if Christ came to other worlds? And what if we could visit them?

And so we feel the same wonder toward Aslan as Christ's contemporaries felt toward Christ: "He's not *safe*. But he's *good*." Aslan is certainly Lewis's supreme literary achievement.

WE FEEL THE SAME WONDER TOWARD ASLAN AS CHRIST'S CONTEMPORARIES FELT TOWARD CHRIST: "HE'S NOT **SAFE**. BUT HE'S **GOOD**."

(2) THE WITCH

Aslan fascinates us to the extent that we are imaginative, good, and healthy minded. The witch, on the other hand, fascinates us only insofar as we have diseased imaginations, morals, or minds. It is not a fault for Lewis to give us a boring witch as the enemy of the fascinating lion, for that is what evil is: boring, uncreative, stereotypical.

THE WITCH FASCINATES US ONLY INSOFAR AS WE HAVE **DISEASED IMAGINATIONS, MORALS,** OR **MINDS.**

(3) THE WARDROBE

But what of the wardrobe? Besides its symbolic association with clothing, it is a door to another world. Why do we find this fascinating and almost credible?

When I once volunteered to teach Sunday school to five-year-olds—by far the hardest teaching job I ever did—my most effective attention-holder was the promise of a chapter of *The Lion, the Witch and the Wardrobe* at the end of each class if they were good. They loved it, of course. But what they loved the most was the wardrobe, the door into Narnia. "Can we find one?" "Why couldn't there be some in our world?" "Did you ever hear of anybody who found one?" And they were not satisfied with any symbolic or allegorical yes. Death, books, *The Lion, the Witch and the Wardrobe* itself, the Bible, other people, and prayer—I tried suggesting all of these as examples of real doors into other worlds. Most of the kids understood, but not one was thrilled. "Oh, is that all it means?" They wanted a real door into Narnia.

And so do I.

The first time I visited The Marion Wade Collection of Lewis items at Wheaton

BESIDES ITS SYMBOLIC ASSOCIATION WITH CLOTHING, IT IS A DOOR TO ANOTHER WORLD.

College in Wheaton, Illinois, many moons ago, the curator was Clyde Kilby, that angel of an English teacher who first made Lewis

known in America. I was duly amazed at Lewis's original handwritten manuscripts for complex and profound books like *The Problem of Pain*; there were hardly any revisions! But what most intrigued me was the wardrobe. There it was, standing like a king in the back of a large room.

Kilby and I were alone in the room. "Is that . . . ?" I stuttered, speechlessly.

"Yes, that's the wardrobe. The very one." Lewis's shabby coat was still hanging in it and his pipe was in its pocket. Both smelled utterly authentic. I had not known that there was a real wardrobe. Wild hope and dreams began to stir.

I looked around for Kilby, to ask a thousand more questions, but he had left the room—with deliberate timing, though I did not know it then. A fire suddenly burned in my heart. I entered the wardrobe, latched the door behind me, and felt behind the coat. Nothing doing. Just an ordinary wooden back. Part of me was not surprised, of course, but another part of me was! Just as I unlatched the door of the wardrobe and poked my head out, Kilby came back into the room. He had known just how much time to leave me.

With a mischievous smile, he said, "I knew you'd do that. Every child under twelve who's ever seen that wardrobe has had to try it."

I didn't feel embarrassed. I almost felt proud. "And you?" I asked.

The elfish smile was his only answer.

Why are we fascinated with passages into other worlds? Surely because they are *other*. All othernesses are fascinating. Birth, death, God, and sex are probably the four most fascinating things in life, for they are all other worlds to us.

We seem to be *designed* for otherness, for wonder and surprise, for exploration of new worlds, not just new data. That's why the most famous passage in the whole history of philosophy is Plato's Cave.

What do we mean by another world?

Not just another *planet*; there are plenty of them. But you can get to them in a rocket ship. You can't get to Narnia that way.

WHY ARE WE FASCINATED WITH PASSAGES INTO OTHER WORLDS? SURELY BECAUSE THEY ARE **OTHER**. ALL OTHERNESSES ARE FASCINATING.

And not just another *dimension*, whether physical (like depth or time) or spiritual (like beauty or value). There are plenty of those other worlds for anyone except the reductionist cynic who commits the fallacy of "nothing-but-tery."

We mean another real created universe. Could there be such things?

I see no reason why not. There is a Creator, and he is incredibly creative. An author writes many books; why couldn't God create many universes?

But if he did, could we get into them? Could there be, in addition to the four real "doors into other worlds" that we mentioned above (birth, death, God, and sex), doors into other worlds like Narnia?

There are no credible stories of real people having gone through real doorways like the wardrobe into real worlds like Narnia. But what does that prove? There were no credible stories of the Boston Red Sox winning the World Series before 2004 either.

Is it so bad to keep looking? To still be twelve years old when you are sixty?

Two people are walking down a street. There is a large stone wall on their left. Both have been down this street many times before. At the next corner they and the wall will both turn left. The first walker knows what he will find in the next minute. The second does not. He holds open the remote but real possibility that he might find an angel. Or a door in that wall that he has never noticed before, a door into something like Narnia.

C. S. Lewis invites us to be that second walker.

Is it so bad to keep looking?
To still be twelve years old
when you are sixty?

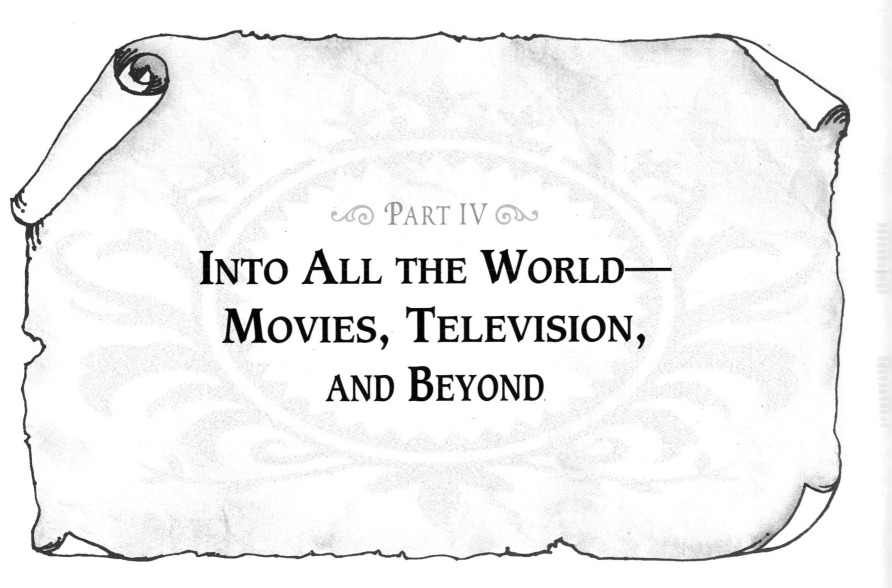

PART IV

INTO ALL THE WORLD—
MOVIES, TELEVISION,
AND BEYOND

Keeping the Wardrobe and all things Lewis safe and secure.

—ROBERT CORDING

JOURNEY:

ONE MAN'S FAITH BRINGS LEWIS'S WORLD TO LIFE

JAMES S. C. BAEHR

Robert Cording is president of Questar Pictures, Inc. and director of The JFP Inspirational Art Collection. Film producer and professional artist with studios in San Diego, California, he has produced and directed more than fifty films and videos including *The Treasure, The Harvest, A Man Without Equal,* and *The Millennial Tribute.*

Robert Cording has proven a faithful philanthropist in bringing the world of C. S. Lewis to life. In March 1983, Cording traveled to Oxford after receiving a flier (forwarded from Lyle Dorsett) advertising the sale of Lewis's old home, The Kilns. Cording stepped into Bucknell and Ballard Realtors and made them an offer they should have refused: $600 down payment for a property worth 95,000 pounds sterling. Miraculously, they accepted Cording's offer: "Later that day, to my amazement, the broker informed me that the owners had agreed and were pleased that the home would be preserved."

"On January 4, 1984, The Kilns officially became the property of The Kilns Association, Limited Partnership," Cording explained, "With the help of Lyle Dorsett of The Wade Center, Paul Ford of The Southern California C. S. Lewis Society, Doug Gresham, stepson of Lewis, and other friends, we had been able to raise the necessary funds for the initial payment on the property." Today, The Kilns property has been beautifully restored and is open throughout the year for visitors by appointment.

Years later Cording paid a visit to The Wade Center at Wheaton College, and found another means to commemorate Lewis. As he spoke with Marj Mead, the associate director of the Center, she noted that "it would be wonderful if we had a painting of Aslan. I know the children would enjoy seeing a picture of the great lion." It was a challenge Cording, a gifted artist, couldn't resist.

"As I began the painting—oils on linen canvas—Aslan, the great noble lion slowly emerged. The 28" x 36" painting is now on display at The Wade Center. I informed Marj and The Wade Center staff that they should be aware that when the lights are turned off at night and everyone has left for the day, it is possible that Aslan leaps out of his frame on the wall and roams through the halls—keeping the Wardrobe and all things Lewis safe and secure."

The Wade Center at Wheaton College.

*T*he greatest irony involved in Lewis's popularity in motion pictures was his own ambivalence towards the film medium. —TERRY LINDVALL

A scene from C. S. Lewis: Beyond Narnia, *a made for TV production for Faith & Values Media that garnered critical acclaim.*

C. S. Lewis at the Cinema

James S. C. Baehr

Lewis portrayed as a young boy in the TV production of C. S. Lewis: Beyond Narnia.

C. S. Lewis's world of Narnia and his own worlds of Oxford and Cambridge have come to life on screen over the course of the last three decades. The tragedy and triumph of Lewis's own life story continues to inspire documentaries and dramatizations years after his death, even while his Narnian tales draw upon past small-screen success and its own deep well of drama in the making of the new Narnia films. Perhaps the greatest irony involved in Lewis's popularity in motion pictures, esteemed Lewis scholar Terry Lindvall suggests, was his own ambivalence towards the film medium, particularly the work of Walt Disney—a current patron of the upcoming Narnia release.

Lewis's Shadow

Lewis's life has spawned several dramatic retellings, including the well-known *Shadowlands* films and several projects currently in the pipeline.

In 1986, the Episcopal Radio-TV Foundation partnered with the BBC to create the first *Shadowlands* film, a made for TV production that garnered critical acclaim. The work was written by William Nicholson and directed by Norman Stone. John O'Connor in the *New York Times* regaled the production: *Shadowlands* moves crisply and runs for only 52 minutes. Yet it manages to be uncommonly moving. The performances are lovely. . . . In its almost unassuming way, *Shadowlands* packs an extraordinary emotional wallop."[1] The movie was shown on PBS, CBS, A&E, and released on videocassette before the end of its run.

How do you tell someone's *L*IFE STORY in 43 minutes? —Norman Stone, filmmaker

Lewis as a young man with his mentor, Professor Kirk, in the TV production of C. S. Lewis: Beyond Narnia.

It also inspired a stage play in 1990 that garnered Nigel Hawthorne the 1992 Tony for best actor on Broadway and a big screen version starring Anthony Hopkins shortly thereafter.[2]

Richard Attenborough's cinematic release of *Shadowlands* also garnered praise. It earned William Nicholson an Oscar nomination for Best Screenplay.[3] *Newsweek* called Hopkins as Lewis "as penetrating as anything he's ever done. . . . It's a wonderfully unlikely, stiff-upper-lip love story. Bring a hanky."[4] Still, some Christian audiences were unsatisfied with the ending of the Hopkins version, where a distraught Lewis appears to have lost faith in his tragic encounter with Joy's death. In reality Lewis's faith proved strengthened and steeled by the deepest questions raised by the death of his beloved, as he discusses extensively in his memoir *A Grief Observed*.

While much of Lewis's life remains untouched by dramatic retelling, new projects currently underway promise to illuminate even more of the beloved Oxbridge scholar's existence. One of the prime catalysts for *Shadowlands* has been Norman Stone, a British filmmaker who shopped the story originally as part of a longer Lewis piece back in the 1980s. I got a chance to sit with Norman and his crew on their last night of shooting the TV special *C. S. Lewis: Beyond Narnia* outside of Oxford, England, in November 2004. "I sort of made a promise to the Old Guy when I got finished [with *Shadowlands*] that I'd come back and do the whole thing . . . 24 years later, I have that chance." Stone's docudrama, created in conjunction with producer Karen Pascal for the Hallmark Channel, focuses on the full arc of Lewis's life and the interplay between his creative work and the philosophy that drove his life. It features interviews with countless top scholars and friends of Lewis but also includes portions of piercing dramatic recreation. "How do you tell someone's life story in 43 minutes?" Stone asks, and answers:

The only way I know is to ask Lewis himself to do it. So I sit Lewis himself in a chair and ask him to look back on his life. . . . Think of it as music, with four different melody lines harmonizing together. You have the experts, Lewis himself telling him his feelings, remembered images, and these dramatized moments. The whole thing blends together into a moving exploration. People have cried reading the script. At the heart of it all is a story. Stories and pictures with truth at the center.

Lewis's experiences in the British private school system were explored in the TV production of C. S. Lewis: Beyond Narnia.

The work of Norman, Karen, and countless others proves that the exploration of Lewis's own life continues, even as his fictional world of Narnia receives unprecedented attention.

NARNIA AT THE CINEMA

Though Lewis's Narnia stories have never before made it to the big screen, they have spawned several widely viewed and much loved television versions. These include both animated and live action productions. If the new Narnia film ends up becoming the great success all predictions claim it will be, it will in large part be due to the positive legacy left by past tellings of Lewis's grand story.

NARNIA ANIMATED

Few lovers of Narnia realize that the 1979 version of *The Lion, the Witch and the Wardrobe* "was the first animated full length movie made for television," according to the Internet Movie Database. "All other previous animated television specials were one hour or less."[5] This television special was created by the Episcopal Radio-TV

Foundation and the Children's Television Workshop. Aired on CBS, the show was watched by thirty-seven million viewers and won an Emmy Award.

Recently, Ted Baehr had the chance to sit down at lunch with Phil Roman and Bill Melendez, two of the animators who worked

Left: Ted Baehr (right) with Bill Melendez, one of the animators who created the characters and also directed the 1979 production of The Lion, the Witch and the Wardrobe. *Below: Melendez with several of his illustrations.*

A LABOR OF LOVE

on the production. Ted worked with Bill on a small portion of *The Lion, the Witch and the Wardrobe* when he was elected president of the organization that produced the television program. Bill directed *The Lion, the Witch and the Wardrobe.*

"It was a labor of love," Bill said about the making of the movie. "Everything about the project appealed to me."

"You figured out a way to do it," Ted told him.

"It was just a good project," Bill replied. "I didn't want to let go of it. It didn't need a lavish production. I wanted to tell the story simply and directly."

"He laid it out and made it very easy for the animators," Phil recalled.

"Bill and Phil saved the project," Ted explained to his companions, because the first director's personal problems kept him from finishing the work. "Bill made it an award-winning program."

Bill believed the key to the program's success was authenticity to the original. "I like to stick to the story and be as precise as I can be," he said. "We do our job as best as we can, but we don't fool around with the premise of the story."

Bill began his work with Walden Media's partner in bringing the newest version of Narnia to fruition: Disney. While at Disney in the 1930s and 1940s, Bill worked on *Bambi, Pinocchio,* and *Dumbo,* arguably some of the greatest animated movies of all time.

Both Phil and Bill said that getting a good story is as essential in animation as it is in live action movies and TV. "The problem of illustrating a story is part of the fun," Bill said. "The hardest thing is sitting down and doing the actual minute drawings of actions and situations."

The new computer technologies in animation (used extensively in the new Narnia films) don't bother Phil as much as animators who prefer hand-drawn cartoons and hand-drawn animated features. "To me, computer technology is just another tool," Phil said. "You still need an animator and a designer."

"I work in a fun industry," Bill concluded, "Everything I do [in animation] turns out to be a lot of fun. It ends up being a happy moment in my life. I've lived a great life." Phil and Bill have also enriched the lives of all those who have enjoyed their animated Narnia.

BBC RENDITION

The BBC and American production company Wonderworks brought to life four of Lewis's seven Narnia Chronicles from 1988 to 1990. The productions included *The Lion, the Witch and the Wardrobe, Prince Caspian* and *The Voyage of the Dawn Treader* (combined), and *The Silver Chair.* The entire set, re-released on DVD in 2002, totals nine hours.

Directed by Marilyn Fox and written by Alan Seymour, the productions follow the book almost word for word. The children are played by Richard Dempsey, Sophie Cook, Jonathon Scott, and Sophie Wilcox.

Though well acted and well liked, the productions suffered from lack of funding. They were filmed for $16 million dollars, a small amount considering their dependence on fantastical sets and epic elements.[6] As Randy Salas of *The Minneapolis Star Tribune* noted in a glowing review,

SKEPTICAL YOUNG VIEWERS WEANED ON TODAY'S GLOSSY FARE MIGHT NOT WANT TO BE BOTHERED BY THIS SIMPLE PRODUCTION. THAT'S TOO BAD, BECAUSE THESE ARE FANTASTIC STORIES VIVIDLY RETOLD.[7]

Other reviewers agreed. Nancy Churnin for Knight Ridder Newspapers claimed, "The heft of the story should pull them in. And once they're in, they just might want to read the books. The books, after all, are the real other-side-of-the-wardrobe, the place where the magical world of Narnia truly awaits."[8]

Fortunately, the small budgets didn't translate into small audiences. By 1988, *The Times of London* noted that 10.6 million British viewers had seen the series.[9] Consistently replayed over the airwaves on both sides of the Atlantic, that number must be exponentially higher today. The numbers who plan to flock to the new *The Lion, the Witch and the Wardrobe* movie could well make it one of the top-earning movies of all time.

WALDEN MEDIA'S AND WALT DISNEY'S NARNIA

The December 2005 release of *The Lion, the Witch and the Wardrobe* by Walden Media and Walt Disney will open the wardrobe door to the next chapter in the history of Narnia, but the project has been years in the making. The success of *The Lord of the Rings* and the Harry Potter franchise no doubt galvanized Disney to pick up the project for distribution. A recent *New York Times* article called the Narnia series "one of the last children's classics unexplored by cinema" and asserted that "the potential rewards are huge" for the company financially. Disney has also enjoyed a partnership deal with Walden Media for several years now, including their dual release of the family film *Holes*. Behind-the-scenes excitement for this project, though, and its spiritual potency and popularity among evangelicals could be portents of an unprecedented release.

FIRST AND FOREMOST, IT WAS EXHILARATING AND A PROFOUND PRIVILEGE TO HAVE THE OPPORTUNITY TO VISIT THE SET OF THIS HISTORY-MAKING FILM. WHEN I GOT DOWN THERE, VIRTUALLY EVERYTHING I WITNESSED AND THE MAJORITY OF THE PEOPLE I WAS IN CONTACT WITH FELT THE SAME THING: THERE IS SOMETHING VERY SPECIAL ABOUT THIS MOVIE, UNLIKE ANYTHING WE'VE EVER BEEN A PART OF. KEEP IN MIND, THESE ARE PROFESSIONALS WITH AN INCREDIBLE RESUME OF SOME OF THE MOST SUCCESSFUL FILMS OF OUR TIME.

—PEB JACKSON, SADDLEBACK CHURCH AND THE PURPOSE-DRIVEN MISSION

I recently spoke with Peb Jackson, who is affiliated with Rick Warren's Saddleback Church and the Purpose-Driven Mission, shortly after his return from the set in New Zealand. "First and foremost, it was exhilarating and a profound privilege to have the opportunity to visit the set of this history-making film. When I got down there," he continued, "virtually everything I witnessed and the majority of the people I was in contact with felt the same thing: there is something very special about this movie, unlike anything we've ever been a part of.

Filming on the movie set of The Lion, the Witch and the Wardrobe *by Walden Media and Walt Disney.*

Filming on the movie set of The Lion, the Witch and the Wardrobe *by Walden Media and Walt Disney.*

Keep in mind, these are professionals with an incredible résumé of some of the most successful films of our time.

Peb attributed this special sense to the broad familiarity that people have with The Chronicles of Narnia, even from childhood. One example is the celebrated director, himself, Andrew Adamson, who was introduced to the books as a young boy by his father who was a missionary in New Guinea.

In spite of rumors of substantial changes to the original text, Jackson stressed his observance of steadfast commitment to the production's authenticity. "There was a tremendous sense of stewardship of the project. There seemed to be a pervasive resolve to be as true to C. S. Lewis's great story as possible. Many people on the set including actors, technicians, and assistant producers were very aware of the millions of Chronicles fans who have high expectations regarding this film. The producer, Mark Johnson, told Peb that even his sixteen-year-old daughter, a fan of The Chronicles said, "Dad, don't mess it up." Jackson also cited that Douglas Gresham's presence on the set, C. S. Lewis's own stepson, was an encouragement that Lewis's vision will be guarded.

Peb also thinks the film could turn viewers toward faith. For many people around the world, the story of Aslan as a Christ figure was the threshold to understanding the gospel.

The Lion, the Witch and the Wardrobe may stand alone in the genre of film in facilitating the realization of God's love and purpose in people's lives. "It's actually thrilling, as a follower of Christ, to think of the potential powerful global influence of this film," said Jackson.

The films success will no doubt lead to sequels. One great irony of that expected success is Lewis's own love/hate relationship with the cinema and Walt Disney, exposed in many of his writings, according to Lewis expert Terry Lindvall.

LEWIS'S LOVE/HATE RELATIONSHIP WITH FILM

Lewis's scholarly passions were largely for a time before his own. As a late medievalist, he relished the world of knights, chivalry, and courtly love. We see glimpses of that passion underneath his Narnia tales; in the knighting of the Pevensie boys, the hunting of the white stag, and the conflict between Narnia and Calormene that can be easily viewed as a crusading conflict between the Christian West and Muslim lands, Lewis's love of the medieval gleams. For such a self-proclaimed "dinosaur" as he, the cinema often proved a modern horror.

This view comes through at several points in The Chronicles, according to Lindvall. "In *The Silver Chair*, it is when she is in

Underland, that Jill remembers the cinema," he writes. "Earlier, Edmund in *The Lion, the Witch and the Wardrobe*, is under the influence of the wicked White Witch. He announces with arrogance and glee that if he were king of Narnia, he would have a 'private cinema.'"[10]

One reason Lewis remained so wary of the film arts was his concern that they diminished imagination. Films would feed to the viewer preprocessed images instead of making them exercise and develop their own imaginative powers. As Lindvall writes, "It would freeze the lively and animated mind of the young viewer with predigested and marketed images of various literary characters and images. It would embalm the vivacious imagination."

Another particularly relevant concern was that the original intentions of the authors were often run roughshod in attempts to make a film more visually dramatic. Lewis went to see a film of H. Rider Haggard's *King Solomon's Mines* at one point. The climax of the book occurs when the protagonists find themselves caught in a subterranean chamber with the threat of death by pitch-black starvation. In the version Lewis viewed, the filmmakers added volcanoes and earthquakes to the scene. Lindvall quotes Lewis's frustration at these changes: "Perhaps the scene in the original was not 'cinematic' and the man was right, by the canons of his own art, in altering it.

ASLAN IS A DIVINE FIGURE, AND ANYTHING REMOTELY APPROACHING THE COMIC WOULD BE TO ME SIMPLE BLASPHEMY.—C. S. LEWIS

Aslan and Howard Berger of KNBEFX, the creator of the mechanical Aslan.

But it would have been better not to have chosen in the first place a story which could be adapted to the screen only by being ruined. Ruined, at least, for me."[11]

These concerns of Lewis echo the concerns of many of his fans as they await the final edit of *The Lion, the Witch and the Wardrobe* film. To Lewis, major alteration of an original text proved ruinous, even to increase cinematic excitement. His oldest fans will no doubt be on guard.

In the greatest of ironies, Lewis proved a particularly forceful critic of Walt Disney, whose childish renditions of the great legends often robbed them of their horrifying vitality. Lindvall notes that "he confessed that he remembered: 'delighting in fairy tales. I fell deeply under the spell of Dwarfs—the old bright-hooded, snowy-bearded dwarfs we had in those days before Arthur Rackham sublimed, or Walt Disney vulgarized, the earthmen.'"[12] Lindvall also recalls "when Jane Douglas, an American actress and playwright, visited him in his rooms to discuss dramatizing *The Lion, the Witch and the Wardrobe*, he responded unyieldingly: "Aslan is a divine figure," he had written on June 19 to discourage her, "and anything remotely approaching the comic (anything in the Disney line) would be to me simple blasphemy."[13] Those who love this divine lion will also be watching this Disney version carefully.

BEYOND

Lewis's concerns about film did not blind him from seeing its power or sensing its possibility. He was hardly wholly critical of the medium. Nor should he have been. Films about Lewis's life and the worlds of his imagination have inspired and empowered viewers everywhere, turning them toward the faith that Lewis himself held sacred. The potency of his imagination, whether expressed through book or film, will continue to transform lives and baptize the imaginations of generations to come.

ENDNOTES:

1. John O'Connor, "'Shadowlands,' a C. S. Lewis Episode," *The New York Times*, 29 October 1986, C26; column 4; cultural desk.
2. John Hartl, "Three Versions, Same Story: Writer Guides 'Shadowlands' from TV to Stage to Film," *The Seattle Times*, 2 January 1994, F8.
3. "1993 Oscar Nominees," *Daily Variety*, 10 February 1994, 20.
4. "A Postgraduate Tearjerker," *Newsweek*, 3 January 1994, 63.
5. http://www.imdb.com/title/tt0079474/?fr=c2l0ZTI1kZnxteD0yMHxsbT0IMDB8dHQ9b258ZmI9dXxwbj0wfHE9bGlvbiwgdGhlIHdpdGNoLCB8aHRtbD0xfG5tbPW9u;fc=3;ft=20;fm=I.
6. *The Advertiser*, 13 September 1990.
7. Randy Salas, "Narnia Comes to Life in BBC Production," *Minneapolis Star Tribune*, 13 September 2002, 22E; variety.
8. Nancy Churnin, "DVD could help kids open wardrobe door to Narnia," *Milwaukee Journal Sentinel*, 22 September 2002, 9E.
9. Valerie Grove, "The Home Service—Watch Without Ma: Interview with Anna Home," *The Times of London*, 27 November 1988, issue 8573.
10. See C. S. Lewis, *The Silver Chair* (New York: Collier, 1970), and C. S. Lewis, *The Lion, the Witch and the Wardrobe* (New York: Collier, 1970), 87.
11. C. S. Lewis, *On Stories* (New York: Harvest Books, 1982), 5–6. In the example of *King Solomon's Mines*, the producer of the film substituted at the climax one kind of danger for another and thereby, for me, ruined the story. But where excitement is the only thing that matters, kinds of danger must be irrelevant. Only degrees of danger will matter. The greater the danger and the narrower the hero's escape from it, the more exciting the story will be. But when we are concerned with the "something else" this is not so, 7.
12. C. S. Lewis, *Surprised by Joy* (New York: Harvest Books, 1955), 54–55.
13. William Griffin, *Clive Staples Lewis: A Dramatic Life* (San Fransisco: Harper and Row, 1986), 360.

The Rules Have Changed for the Better:

The Chronicles of Narnia Games

Lili Baehr

ack when my husband, Ted, was president of the organization that produced *The Lion, the Witch and the Wardrobe* for CBS Television, he was inspired to create a series of games that required cooperation rather than competition to win.

After diligent research, he came across the top game inventor Paul Gruen, who was the only living game producer with three of the top-ten-selling games to his credit. Ted asked Paul if he could help Ted design a game where a person would have to help the other players to move forward.

After much brainstorming, they did just that. The Chronicles of Narnia games The Lion and the White Witch and The Voyage of the Dawn Treader were released. They became and remained a huge success for many years.

Children playing the board game, The Lion and the White Witch.

When we forge ahead into the unfamiliar, although we will face trials, we should find that blessings will follow.

THE CHILDREN DISCOVER NARNIA

INSPIRATIONAL MOMENTS FOR REFLECTION: FURTHER UP AND FURTHER IN

TED BAEHR AND PEIRCE BAEHR

Narnia Beckons aims to help you grow in grace, faith, and wisdom. In this chapter we are reflecting on the truth that compelled C. S. Lewis—the gospel of Jesus Christ. We pray that the brief reflections that follow will bless you in wonderful ways. Please note that these reflections are inspired by the chapters in *The Lion, the Witch and the Wardrobe* but do not always follow the chapter titles in Lewis's book. Although we use his titles for section headings, these reflections often develop from some of the spiritual subplots and themes in the chapters.

REFLECTION ON CHAPTER 1:
LUCY LOOKS INTO THE WARDROBE

INTO THE UNKNOWN

A good story starts in the middle, not the beginning. It starts with something at stake,

with a bang, when crisis hits. C. S. Lewis begins *The Lion, the Witch and the Wardrobe* in this way with the Pevensie children, Peter, Susan, Edmund, and Lucy, sent away from home into an unfamiliar world.

Like the Pevensie children, we have all, at one time or another, been sent into the unfamiliar. God actually mandates such an adventure by commanding us to go into all the world to spread the good news. When the fearful early Christians would not leave the temple to go into the world to proclaim the good news of Jesus Christ, God himself drove them out into the world to fulfill his Great Commission.

In a similar way, although they make plans to explore the outdoors, "circumstances" drive the Pevensie children to the spare room with the wardrobe that sometimes opens into Narnia. Edmund grumbles about the change of plans, but Lucy, the youngest, forges ahead through the fur coats in the wardrobe into the land of Narnia.

When we choose to forge ahead into the unfamiliar, although we will face trials, we should find, as Lucy and the early Christians did, that blessings follow.

QUESTIONS AND REFLECTIONS

Think of a time when you were sent out into the unfamiliar.

How did it affect you?

How did you respond?

Do you see God's direction in your life? If not, why not?

Reflect on a time you did see God clearly through uncertain times.

Read Psalm 91.

Prayer: Father, sometimes we are sent out into the unfamiliar, where it is easy to feel alienated and alone. Please be with us as you have promised and help us to trust you on the journey that we may have strength even in difficulty to complete the tasks before us.

REFLECTION ON CHAPTER 2:
WHAT LUCY FOUND THERE

INNOCENCE AND NAÏVETÉ

Lucy enters the land of Narnia in innocence, and her innocence helps her find the good in Narnia and survive the bad.

Often when we discover the spiritual realm, the first thing we find is not a sugar-coated world but rather a complex parallel universe where things are not as they appear. In certain parts of the spiritual universe, the dark forces of the adversary hold sway over even the nicest of companions.

Lucy finds a faun, Mr. Tumnus, who is not all he seems. He is tempted to serve the evil white witch. Having tea with him, Lucy almost succumbs to his enchantments that are intended to deliver her to the witch.

Lucy's innocence is almost naïve, and while Jesus in Matthew 18:3 calls us to be innocent, "I assure you . . . unless you . . . become like children, you will never enter

the kingdom of heaven," Jesus does not commend being naïve. In fact, he tells us in Matthew 10:16, "Look, I'm sending you out like sheep among wolves. Therefore be as shrewd as serpents and as harmless as doves."

Naïveté is susceptible to temptation. Christian innocence seeks out wisdom and discernment to make the right choices. Tumnus, himself, is naïve about the existence of the sons of Adam and daughters of Eve and corrupted by his fear of the white witch. Yet, when he discovers Lucy's kind innocence, he repents, knowing it may cost him everything.

QUESTIONS AND REFLECTIONS

To distinguish between innocence and naïveté, reflect on a time when you unwittingly found yourself in a harmful situation (for example, at an unhealthy movie with friends). Did you respond by seeking wisdom and by using discernment in order to retain innocence? If you did not, what prevented or seduced you?

Consider a time when your innocence did shield or help you through a difficult or tempting situation. Consider also the reverse, when you fell into temptation. What made the difference?

As humans, we all have mixed records for resisting temptation. The key is to return to

God when we fall and use discernment and wisdom to resist and avoid those things that would trap us.

Read Psalm 23.

Prayer: Father, we know you are with us and that all things work together for the good of those who love you. Still we are often naive and susceptible to temptation of many sorts. Please help us understand your Word and your guidelines so we can have the wisdom and discernment to avoid temptation. Surround us with your grace and lead us to make the choices that please you.

REFLECTION ON CHAPTER 3:
EDMUND AND THE WARDROBE

HOLDING ON TO THE TRUTH

If you have prayed for the impossible or encountered the unbelievable, you have probably noticed that a miracle seems less of a miracle after it happens. If you have prayed for someone who is incurably sick and that person recovers, before recovery the healing appears impossible. After recovery plausible explanations abound: the medicine, a misdiagnosis, or a misconception could be the source of the cure.

Just so, when Lucy comes out of the

wardrobe, her journey into the parallel, spiritual world of Narnia, appears to be a figment of her imagination. The hours she spent in Narnia took no time in the real world, and the wardrobe no longer leads into a different universe.

Unlike Lucy, whose innocence and honesty help her keep to the truth that she had been in Narnia, many people soon doubt or forget their experiences of the miraculous and the other. Rather than give in to doubt in the face of unbelief, we must hold on to

the truth and continue to seek God's presence so we may not forget him. Lucy was rebuffed by her siblings and the circumstances, but she holds the course and finds her way back to Narnia.

Knowing how fleeting human memory is, God often urged the children of Israel to remember how he brought them out of Egypt, through the wilderness, to the promised land. He urged Israel to remember the miracles that were the signs of his presence in their lives. The Latin root for the word miracle is *sign*, and the signs he gave them, and those he gives us, will lead the way to his eternal Kingdom.

QUESTIONS AND REFLECTIONS

Have you ever been so challenged by the world, the flesh, or the devil that you doubted your experience with the truth?

In the face of doubt, what evidences in your life point to God's presence and work?

Read Deuteronomy 7 and Mark 8:1–21.

Prayer: Father, forgive us for forgetting your miraculous signs that we have experienced in answer to our prayers. Help us remember the times we have seen you at work in our lives that we may hold the course and know you more fully. May your face shine upon us as we live out our lives for your glory in expectation of the eternal kingdom.

REFLECTION ON CHAPTER 4:

TURKISH DELIGHT

༃

SELFISHNESS LEADS TO
SELF-DESTRUCTION

C. S. Lewis believed gluttony was one of the worst sins because it was the root of other sins. When Edmund enters Narnia, he does not like the witch, until she gives him what he thinks he desires: Turkish delight. As soon as he begins eating the Turkish delight, he craves more and is willing to tell the witch anything to get what he desires. At the same time Edmund starts to think how important he is and, in his selfishness, elevates himself above his brother and sisters. Eventually, when he reunites with Lucy, he betrays the truth out of his selfish lust for more candy (despite the fact he has eaten so much it sickens him).

Edmund seems vile in this chapter, but, in fact, he expresses characteristics common to all of us. At different times we all become gluttonous for something, be it food, or things, or experiences, or time; and we betray those around us for the sake of feeding our lusts. Further, these lusts contribute to our pride in life because we rationalize that we are better or more deserving or more needy than others. In our materially wealthy world, these afflictions of gluttony are all the more intense in the face of spiritual confusion. Our difficult task is to put our desires in perspective and seek not our own will but the will of God—a thing Edmund, in this chapter, proved unable to do.

QUESTIONS AND REFLECTIONS

When you are taken by a desire for something, how often do you consider the impact of your actions on others? How often do you put yourself at the center of the equation?

Consider a time you stuffed yourself with too much of something and felt bad because of it. How could you respond better in the future? Think over your lifestyle: What tend to be the strongest lusts in your life? How might those lusts hurt others as well as yourself? Edmund is every man and every woman. He needs to be filled with the grace of God so he can withstand the temptations of the world, the flesh, and the devil. When he accepts the grace that God wants to give him, he will become humble and wise, but until then his gluttony blinds him to the needs of others.

Read I John 2:15.

Prayer: Father, forgive us for often falling into gluttony. We are easily distracted by our lust for things and all too readily place our wants over the needs of others. Have mercy on us and fill us with your loving grace that we may stand against our own selfishness and love our neighbors as we ought.

Reflection on Chapter 5:
Back on This Side of the Door

⁓

Breaking the Bonds of Selfishness

When Lucy shares her joy at rediscovering Narnia with Edmund, Edmund does the meanest thing: he lies to steal her joy and make himself superior. In Hollywood there are those who contend that the primary motivation of the top men and women in the media is not fame or fortune but Schadenfreude, taking pleasure in other people's failures. Regrettably, it is not only the person responsible, like Edmund, who indulges in Schadenfreude; often many people, including friends and family, find pleasure in the failure of others. In Lucy's case Peter and Susan are convinced by Edmund to look down on Lucy and dismiss her claims.

To avoid indulging in Schadenfreude because of pride or envy, we must be discerning. In this chapter, the professor helps Lucy's siblings gain discernment through logic. He helps her siblings analyze the various possibilities regarding the veracity of Lucy's story in a way that ultimately gives credence to Lucy's claims regarding Narnia.

The key to the professor's technique is asking the right questions and analyzing the answers. This process helps us to make wise decisions and avoid jumping to conclusions.

Questions and Reflections

Consider how often the media indulges in Schadenfreude toward the famous or powerful. Think of a time you gloated over another's downfall. Was that action helpful or demeaning to you? How? How did it make you feel? Reflect on a time when someone took pleasure in your failure or dismissed what you know to be the truth for the wrong reasons. How did you respond?

Read Matthew 7.

Prayer: Father, forgive us for jumping to conclusions and taking pleasure in the failures of others. Help us ask the right questions and seek understanding so we may see things as you do, with love and compassion placing others above ourselves.

Reflection on Chapter 6:

Into the Forest

Attitude Not Circumstance

When the four children are forced to hide in the wardrobe to avoid the housekeeper's tour of the professor's home, they discover that there is a Narnia, thus proving that Lucy was telling the truth. Then, when Edmund directs them to the lamppost, they realize that he had lied to them about not visiting Narnia before, as Lucy had claimed. Lucy is affirmed while Edmund is exposed.

We have all been affirmed at times, just when it seemed our cause was lost. And, although we may protest in public that this couldn't be me, we have all been exposed at times when we lied to puff ourselves up or to put down someone else. The question is not the affirmation of our righteousness or the exposing of our flaws and faults but how we react to being justified or exposed.

With regard to affirmation, are we humble and gracious to those who were proved wrong? Or do we become prideful and lord our victory over them, saying, "We told you so"?

With regard to being exposed or caught in the act of lying, covering up, or dissembling, are we humble enough to apologize and determine not to engage in such behavior again according to the best of our ability by God's grace? Or do we do what Edmund did and retire into ourselves, waiting for the moment to reassert our superiority or, even worse, to get revenge?

Grace and humility are not easy. We need to realize that we can forgive and be forgiven because Jesus suffered and died to forgive us. Often the other party will not forgive or will not be forgiven themselves, so we have an even more difficult time living out our faith in the forgiveness that we have received from God.

Have you ever been vindicated on a major issue? Did you accept your victory humbly with grace?

Have you ever been found out lying about something that seemed plausible and beyond question? Did you react with humble repentance? Did you determine to change or seek revenge?

Read Romans 2:1–4.

Prayer: Father, forgive us for feeling superior and self-righteous when we are vindicated and for feeling resentful and vengeful when we are wrong. Have mercy on us, most merciful Father, and fill us with your Holy Spirit so that we may humbly walk in your ways and not our own.

REFLECTION ON CHAPTER 7:
A DAY WITH THE BEAVERS

THE NAME ABOVE ALL NAMES

There are moments in life when we are touched by the sense of the other—the unknown, the extraordinary—in the midst of the ordinary. Such is the case when the Pevensie children hear the name of Aslan for the first time. They sense the import of the name of Aslan even though they have never heard it before. They know that it has meaning just as if they had experienced the true meaning of the name in a dream long ago. This sense of awe and mystery and the ordinary yet extraordinary pervades chapter 7.

In each of our lives, there are moments that are pregnant with meaning when we are able to sense but not quite decipher. These are the moments when the knowledge of God and his grace are close to us. They are, in a sense, obtuse moments because if we look directly at them, the meaning disappears.

It is important at those times to listen without trying to interpret, to let God speak to you without trying to shape what he says to your will.

QUESTIONS AND REFLECTIONS

Have you ever encountered the extraordinary in such a way that it seemed ordinary? Have you ever felt awe?

When God directs you, how often do you allow him to speak without trying to conform his words to your presumptions and prejudices?

Those moments are like being surprised by joy.

Read Matthew 13:10–17.

Prayer: Father, you alone are holy, apart, and unique. Please shine your countenance upon us that we may experience your presence and hear your voice. Forgive us for trying to fit you into a box. Help us rest in you and enjoy your presence in our lives.

Reflection on Chapter 8:
What Happened After Dinner
Grace Not Works

No matter how much Lucy, Peter, and Susan want to help Mr. Tumnus, Mr. Beaver tells them there is nothing they can do. He even tells them, "It is no good your trying. . . . But now that Aslan is on the move—" Suddenly, they are swept up in the good news that the king, the lord of the whole wood, the son of the great emperor-beyond-the-sea, the fulfillment of all the prophecies, who isn't safe but is good, is coming to rescue Narnia. Even though they are swept up in expectation, they still want to do something but are told that all they can do is wait to meet him.

When we are at wit's end and hope has run out on us, we learn then that there is real hope; there is fulfillment of prophecy. The son of the Creator of the universe comes to rescue us, and we have to do nothing except welcome him. What great news! The Creator in the flesh came and comes to save us.

The story of *The Lion, the Witch and the Wardrobe* does not end there because the coming of Aslan is the beginning of making all things new. Just so, the story of our salvation does not end with Jesus Christ, because his coming, his death, and his resurrection initiate the beginning of making all things new on Earth.

Questions and Reflections

The last time you were at your wit's end, did you realize the value of hope? On what do you usually place your hope?

Have you ever felt completely unable to help others or yourself? Knowing that God is always with his children, we must learn to trust him, especially in our helplessness. Sometimes we are called to wait.

Read Romans 8:18–30.

Prayer: Father, when we reach the end of ourselves and all hope seems lost, may we know you who alone can save through your son, Jesus Christ. We ask you to save us and our family and friends because you, the Holy One, are our only hope.

Reflection on Chapter 9:
In the Witch's House

Whom Shall We Serve

The name of Aslan brings joy to the three Pevensie children who are thinking of helping another; but for Edmund, who is thinking about Turkish delight, the name of Aslan engenders a horrible feeling. So he sets off to the witch's castle, only to find that the way is cold and lonely, and the reception is not what he expected. Edmund finds there is a price to pay for gluttony.

The Word of God asks each of us to choose life or death (Deut. 30:19), to choose whom we shall serve. Edmund chooses to serve his stomach, and by doing so he relegates himself to serving the white witch.

Every one of us has made the mistake of choosing to serve our lusts, our greed, our envy, or our jealousy over God's will. Thus, we have all found ourselves on the road to serfdom, on the road to serving powers that at first appear benign but soon reveal themselves to be evil and destructive. At that point we, like Edmund, are truly lost. However, no one is beyond the love of God, no matter how much he or she is blinded by self-deception, as Edmund soon finds out.

Questions and Reflections

The last time you were confronted with a choice between satisfying your selfish lusts and following God's path, how did you handle the situation? If you chose your lusts, did you soon find it a poor trade-off, like selling your soul for a bit of Turkish delight?

Have you ever felt yourself trapped by the wrong choices you have made?

Read Romans 1.

Prayer: Father, you are the only way, the truth, and the life. Please forgive us for choosing our ways and putting our desires above yours. Forgive us also for trusting the world's offer of fame, fortune, or happiness when such things are nothing but dross without you.

Reflection on Chapter 10:
The Spell Begins to Break

Eternal Gifts

As soon as Mr. Beaver realizes that Edmund is a traitor, he hurries everyone out of his home to find Aslan and avoid being found by the white witch. While hiding and traveling, they discover that Christmas is coming and that Narnia is beginning to thaw. They realize that the witch's spell is being overturned by the return of Aslan. Furthermore, they meet Father Christmas, who gives each of them the gifts they most need.

Some (like Lewis's good friend J. R. R. Tolkien) have questioned why Father Christmas is in C. S. Lewis's book, but Father Christmas is merely an ambassador who brings gifts that have tremendous spiritual significance. These gifts not only help the children in time of need but also teach them about their own strengths and weaknesses.

Just so, God bestows gifts and talents upon each of us that help us in time of need and instruct us about whose we are. God is not fickle. He doesn't take back the gifts and talents he bestows upon us. But we can use those gifts and talents for good or for ill. God gave President Lincoln the gift of public speaking, and he used it for good, while Hitler perverted his gift to enslave and destroy millions.

QUESTIONS AND REFLECTIONS

Looking over your life, what gifts and talents has God given you?

How have you used your talents for good? For ill?

The good news is that he longs for you to use them properly and will come to your aid whenever you ask. Even better is that beyond the gifts and talents he gives us, by submitting to his Spirit, he gives us incredible fruit: "love, joy, peace, patience, kindness, goodness, faithfulness, gentleness, and self-control" (Gal. 5:22–23 NIV).

Read: Galatians 5.

Prayer: Father, we are eternally grateful for the gifts that you bestow on us. May we use them wisely to glorify you and bless others. In so doing, help us grow in the fruit of the Spirit: "love, joy, peace, patience, kindness, goodness, faithfulness, gentleness, and self-control." And, Father, forgive us for those times when we have misused your gifts and perverted our talents for our own end. Praise you and thank you, Lord, for your great goodness.

REFLECTION ON CHAPTER *11*:
ASLAN IS NEARER
PROMISES, PROMISES

While Mr. and Mrs. Beaver are leading the other children to Aslan, Edmund is discovering the eternal truth that temptation is not what it appears to be. The white witch, like her real-life counterpart, the devil, promises far more than

Sex, fame, and fortune can be equally unfulfilling. Real stories abound of famous misers, such as John Paul Getty, who died in fear of poverty, or horrible dictators, such as Joseph Stalin, who starved to death because he was so fearful of everyone around him.

Temptations are often just a mirage leading further into the desert where you find yourself without those things really needed for life.

QUESTIONS AND REFLECTIONS

Think of a time you followed temptation only to discover it promised more than it delivered. Considering temptation's legacy of dissatisfaction, it is a wonder we repeatedly fall prey to it so easily. The good news is there is always a choice. As Edmund discovered, spring is coming; Aslan is at hand. For us, we need only ask and we will be saved.

Read I Corinthians 10.

Prayer: Father, forgive us for falling prey to the tempter and temptation. We have too often sought fame, fortune, or worldly happiness only to find it never satisfies. In fact, such things only lead deeper into darkness. Please have mercy on us and deliver us that we may choose the good. Fill us with your Spirit and let all that we do glorify you because in you we find true fulfillment.

she delivers. In fact, part of what she promises Edmund—to make him a prince—is merely a poor second to what Aslan has already destined him to be—a king.

Just so, temptations in real life almost always turn out to be far less than they promised. Alcohol and drugs promise momentary freedom from the trials of life but always deliver much less. One can hardly hope that the next venture into the bottle will deliver what it promises when the initial experience offers little more than muddled thinking and strained relationships.

REFLECTION ON CHAPTER *12*:
PETER'S FIRST BATTLE
FACE-TO-FACE

Though they are told there is nothing they can do, Aslan sends Peter into lone battle against one of the white witch's feared wolves so he can grow in courage and wisdom and become a king of Narnia.

The battle against the wolf is not the only challenge Peter must face in this chapter. He must come face-to-face with the lord of Narnia, the great lion Aslan, and admit that his anger toward his brother was partially responsible for Edmund's treachery.

In our walk with Jesus, we will face more than trials; we also will come face-to-face with our Lord and confess our sins, our wrongheaded attitudes toward neighbors, friends, and family. Sometimes, like Peter, we are so convinced of our goodness and our righteousness that we ignore the impact of our bad attitude on others. Therefore, God tells us in Luke 6:37–42 to beware judging others lest we fall prey to the same temptations.

QUESTIONS AND REFLECTIONS

Dealing with hypocrisy, have you ever judged another and found yourself doing the thing you condemned the other person for doing?

Have you ever gotten angry at someone you loved only to drive that person into deeper hurt and sin? How, if ever, where you able to resolve your sin?

We all are hypocrites at times. Like Peter, when we realize our hypocrisy, we need to come face-to-face with our Lord and confess our sins. The good news is that he does forgive us and sends us forth as more than conquerors in Jesus Christ.

Read Luke 6:20–36.

Prayer: Father, thank you for loving and forgiving us in spite of our sinful brokenness. Help us forgive others and ourselves as you have forgiven us. May we be kind, loving, and understanding toward others so that we may manifest your love to all people at all times.

REFLECTION ON CHAPTER 13:
DEEP MAGIC FROM THE DAWN OF TIME

FULFILLING THE LAW

In this chapter Aslan submits to the law of God or (in the terms of the book) to the deep magic of the emperor. He knows that he must fulfill the deep magic in order that Edmund might be saved.

Many people have looked at the good news of the New Testament and dismissed justice and law as having passed away. Heaven and earth may pass away, but the law is part of God's grace. Just as obeying the deep magic of the emperor was necessary to free Edmund, so by fulfilling God's law Jesus Christ saves us.

Furthermore, the law itself protects the poor and weak from the powerful and mighty who would use strength to steal from those in need. To this end, in the Bible the law protects Naboth and his meager possession from the avaricious King Ahab and his wife Jezebel. When Ahab breaks the law, he is condemned by God (see 2 Kings 9:26).

Questions and Reflections

Consider how the benefits of God's law are part of God's grace. The two require each other.

Have you a clear understanding of why Jesus Christ needed to fulfill the law of God by dying for our sins?

The good news is that we now live in him through grace with his law written on our hearts, the law of love for our neighbor and our God.

Read Romans 3.

Prayer: Father, thank you for your gift of salvation and the grace you freely pour out on us. Thank you also for our adoption as your children through the death and resurrection of your son, our Savior, Jesus Christ. We are grateful for your law that calls each of us to love you with heart, mind, soul, and strength and to love our neighbors as ourselves.

Reflection on Chapter 14:
The Triumph of the Witch
&
The Passion of Aslan

Up to this point in film history, Mel Gibson's movie *The Passion of the Christ* is the most powerful motion picture presentation of the suffering Jesus endured on the way to the cross (though there have been more than 120 movies featuring Christ's life and passion). In literature, Aslan's climb to the stone table, while enduring mocking by the white witch's rabble of monsters and death at the hand of the witch, delivers the same level of emotional punch.

Most of the power in this chapter comes from our identification with Lucy and Susan's vulnerability as they watch Aslan's suffering and sacrifice. Susan and Lucy's emotional involvement evokes our emotional involvement. Just as they want to help Aslan and cannot, so we often want to help and can do nothing.

C. S. Lewis must have felt something similar watching his wife Joy suffer and die. I have felt something similar watching my wife suffer (from ten years of chemotherapy).

Aslan's suffering and death are much more intense, of course, because it is not just death but the cruelty of mocking and torture at the hands of the evil witch. And Jesus Christ's suffering is immeasurably more than that.

However, even in the midst of witnessing such evil, we must not despair. God is in control, and he has told us the ending—an ending that is the essence of good news.

Questions and Reflections

Have you ever been caught up in the trials of a loved one and been unable to help? Could you hope in Christ despite the pain?

We are called to have faith even in the darkest hour and not to grow faint or join with the cynics and the mockers.

Read Matthew 27.

Prayer: Father, help us to feel your presence in our darkest hours. Stand by us that we may know you and the trials you went through for the sake of all humankind. Father, you are always faithful, and we love you.

Reflection on Chapter 15: Deeper Magic from Before the Dawn of Time

Resurrection Power

In the midst of their grief, Lucy and Susan experience resurrection power. Aslan comes back to life—larger, more beautiful, and more powerful than before. He willingly lay down his life for the traitor Edmund, and the law of the emperor written before the dawn of time provided that "when a willing victim who had committed no treachery was killed in a traitor's stead, the Table would crack and Death itself would start working backward." Suddenly Lucy and Susan are caught up in a tremendous romp with the son of the emperor himself, for he is alive and he is real!

Just so, Jesus was crucified for our sins and was resurrected into new life. He appeared to his disciples and ate with them and comforted them. His death ripped open the veil in the temple so that all humankind could stand in the presence of God, and it gave us victory over death itself.

We have been adopted into his kingdom to share his celebration banquet. Too many of us, however, wait outside the banquet hall, milling around, afraid to partake. He calls on us to share his kingdom with him and to spread the good news of his victory over sin and death.

QUESTIONS AND REFLECTIONS

Have you felt the exhilaration of new life with Jesus Christ? If not, you are missing the Christian promise.

Many of us forget the joy of our first experience of his overcoming grace. When we do, we should look at his empty tomb and consider his victory to remember afresh his love and be assured that he reigns forever.

Read John 20–21.

Prayer: Father, we rejoice in the resurrection of your son, our Savior, Jesus Christ. Thank you for adopting us as your children and letting us share in Christ's inheritance and the eternal victory celebration. We pray for your help to spread the good news to all the world.

REFLECTION ON CHAPTER 16: WHAT HAPPENED ABOUT THE STATUES

THE BREATH OF LIFE

Many of us have been frozen with fear, trapped in the clutches of darkness. In this chapter Aslan breathes on the animals and people whom the white witch turned to stone, and his breath brings new life to the frozen multitude.

Then the reborn group goes forth to battle the white witch, filled with Aslan's breath and equipped with the gifts he has given them.

Just so, Jesus breathed on his disciples in John 20:22 to give them his Holy Spirit and thus empower them to go into all the world and spread the good news of his kingdom. At Pentecost God poured out his Holy Spirit again to equip his people for the work he had given them.

Think back to a time when you first felt God's presence, his breath of life. Are you still walking in that victorious new life? If not, what changed?

You need only ask for reconnection with God, and you shall receive.

Read Acts 2.

Prayer: Father, thank you for living within us through your Holy Spirit. Fill us afresh with your Spirit that we may exhibit true life. Thank you for being our strength and making us more than conquerors in order to go throughout the world and set the captives free. Accompany us on the adventure that you have set before us.

REFLECTION ON CHAPTER 17:
THE HUNTING OF THE WHITE STAG

৯

INTO ALL THE WORLD

In this chapter the Pevensies reign as kings and queens on the thrones Aslan destined for them. Although they live in victory, they must continue to ride out in power to rid the world of the remnants of the white witch's army. Furthermore, they are called to enact just laws and govern wisely.

God has appointed his people to live in victory and govern wisely. He has given us the opportunity to expand his reign. And, he has set us on a wonderful adventure to follow him as his ambassadors further up and further in.

Seek him. Seek his will. Follow his leading. Let him take you further. Let go and let God take over your life.

At the very end of the story, the professor tells the Pevensie children that "once a king in Narnia, always a king in Narnia." Just so, once an adopted son or daughter of God, always an heir of his kingdom, reigning with him in power and might.

QUESTIONS AND REFLECTIONS

Do not forget who you are in Jesus Christ.

Do not forsake your inheritance.

He loved you so much that he gave his only begotten son that you might have life more abundantly. Now, take hold of that promise.

Read Acts 1:4–8.

Prayer: Father, we know you call us into your kingdom and empower us to do your will.

Still today we need him to pour out his Holy Spirit on us and free us from fear. Even so, we are weak vessels who often lose sight of the victory he has given us. We must remember that in his Holy Spirit we are more than conquerors. He won the victory for us on the cross. He has given us new life in Jesus Christ. We can go into all the world to set the captives free.

We thank you that we may know you face-to-face. We thank you for the wit and wisdom of C. S. Lewis and the seeds of understanding that you plant in our hearts through his work *The Lion, the Witch and the Wardrobe.* We know that as Narnia beckons, you beckon us into your kingdom. We choose to follow you daily into the true life of abundance and grace.

ONCE A KING IN NARNIA, ALWAYS A KING IN NARNIA.

The Chronicles of Narnia will beckon you into the kingdom of God, where you will find true rest and grace.

THE RESURRECTION OF ASLAN

ONLY THE BEGINNING OF THE ADVENTURES OF NARNIA

And as they were saying these things, He Himself stood among them. He said to them, "Peace to you!" But they were startled and terrified and thought they were seeing a ghost. "Why are you troubled?" He asked them. "And why do doubts arise in your hearts? Look at My hands and My feet, that it is I Myself! Touch Me and see, because a ghost does not have flesh and bones as you can see I have." Having said this, He showed them His hands and feet. But while they still could not believe because of [their] joy and were amazed, He asked them, "Do you have anything here to eat?" So they gave Him a piece of a broiled fish, and He took it and ate in their presence.

Then He told them, "These are My words that I spoke to you while I was still with you—that everything written about Me in the Law of Moses, the Prophets, and the Psalms must be ful-filled." Then He opened their minds to understand the Scriptures. He also said to them, "This is what is written: the Messiah would suffer and rise from the dead the third day, and repentance for forgiveness of sins would be proclaimed in His name to all the nations, begin-ning at Jerusalem. You are witnesses of these things. And look, I am sending you what My Father promised. As for you, stay in the city until you are empowered from on high." (Luke 24:36–49)

Narnia Beckons: C. S. Lewis's The Lion, the Witch and the Wardrobe and Beyond is only the beginning of your journeys in Narnia. C. S. Lewis's writings will open up the curtain wide and help you to know the truth, so you can make him known. Better still, The Chronicles of Narnia will beckon you into the kingdom of God, where you will find true rest and grace.

Lewis called The Chronicles of Narnia a "supposal." These books are not pure alle-gory, nor do these books avoid allegorical allusions. Rather, The Chronicles of Narnia suppose an alternate universe where the Creator appears in a unique form to save the people of that world.

As shown by his last interview with Sherwood Wirt in this book, C. S. Lewis was an orthodox mere Christian. However, minor questions of theology arise about his Chronicles of Narnia series if his books are taken out of the context of the entire corpus of his writings after he came to a saving knowledge of Jesus Christ. Therefore, although *The Lion, the Witch and the Wardrobe* appears to Christian eyes as explicitly Christian, it must not be used as a theological text, just as the rest of the books in The Chronicles of Narnia do not lend themselves to being theological texts.

The Chronicles of Narnia were written as children's books, and C. S. Lewis himself was reluctant to be too drawn out about the meaning of Narnia, preferring, as he put it, to "steal past those watchful dragons" of the church and the world that often frighten off those who might otherwise be exposed to the gospel.

In this regard, Dr. Peter Kreeft's insight is helpful: "How did Lewis succeed? By creeping past what Walter Hooper called the two 'watchful dragons' of duty and familiarity, which inhibit our heart's spontaneous response of fascination. No one in the Gospels who ever met Him was bored—not His friends, not His enemies, not those who couldn't figure out whether to be His friends or His enemies. The word repeatedly used for the reaction of all three groups is *thaumadzein*, 'wonder,' 'amazement,' 'fascination.' *All* familiar categories failed to contain Him. He took everyone off their guard."

It is important to realize that beyond *The Lion, the Witch and the Wardrobe* every Christian is called to know God and make him known because we love God and our neighbor. This is the essence of theology: knowing God to make him known to rescue the lost and hurting from self-destruction. God has no grandchildren, and so it is up to us to communicate the good news of salvation to all humankind. C. S. Lewis did just that in many wonderful ways, including The Chronicles of Narnia.

While C. S. Lewis was *a* master of communication, Jesus is *the* master of communication. His dramatic parable word picture supposals are as pertinent today as they were two thousand years ago. He understood the power of communication and how ideas shape civilizations. His Word transformed one of the most powerful civilizations in history, the Roman Empire, and continues to transform the world today.

As in The Chronicles of Narnia book *The Last Battle*, there is a war raging around us, but not the one on the news. Rather, the war is a spiritual war being fought for the hearts and souls of each human being. The victory in this war is only to be found in Jesus Christ.

In all of this, it is important to remember that God is sovereign; we are more than conquerors in Jesus Christ, and God gives us the victory. In fact, this is the essence of the good news that we need not despair and can rest and rejoice in him. "Rejoice in the Lord always. I will say it again: Rejoice! Let your gentleness be evident to all. The Lord is near. Do not be anxious about anything, but in everything, by prayer and petition, with thanksgiving, present your requests to God. And the peace of God, which transcends all understanding, will guard your hearts and your minds in Christ Jesus" (Phil. 4:4–7 NIV).

To go deeper and for more great articles, insights, information, and reflections by some of the best C. S. Lewis scholars, please go to www.movieguide.org. With proof of purchase of *Narnia Beckons*, you will be able to access more great articles and insights into *The Lion, the Witch and the Wardrobe*.

For more information, call or write:
MOVIEGUIDE®
2510-G Las Posas Rd.
Camarillo, CA 93010
805-383-2000 tel.
805-383-4089 fax
www.movieguide.org
(800) 899-6684

HOW DID LEWIS SUCCEED?

By creeping past what Walter Hooper called the two "watchful dragons" of duty and familiarity, which inhibit our heart's spontaneous response of fascination. No one in the Gospels who ever met Him was bored—not His friends, not His enemies, not those who couldn't figure out whether to be His friends or His enemies. The word repeatedly used for the reaction of all three groups is *thaumadzein*, "wonder," "amazement," "fascination." All familiar categories failed to contain Him. He took everyone off their guard.

—Dr. Peter Kreeft

He who testifies about these things
says, "Yes, I am coming quickly."
Amen! Come, Lord Jesus!
The grace of the Lord Jesus be with
all the saints. Amen.

—REVELATION 22:20–21